CULTURE SMART!

SAUDI ARABIA

Nicholas Buchele

·K·U·P·E·R·A·R·D·

First published in Great Britain 2008
by Kuperard, an imprint of Bravo Ltd
59 Hutton Grove, London N12 8DS
Tel: +44 (0) 20 8446 2440   Fax: +44 (0) 20 8446 2441
www.culturesmartguides.com
Inquiries: sales@kuperard.co.uk

Culture Smart! is a registered trademark of Bravo Ltd

Distributed in the United States and Canada
by Random House Distribution Services
1745 Broadway, New York, NY 10019
Tel: +1 (212) 572-2844   Fax: +1 (212) 572-4961
Inquiries: csorders@randomhouse.com

Series Editor Geoffrey Chesler
Design Bobby Birchall

ISBN 978 1 85733 351 0

British Library Cataloguing in Publication Data
A CIP catalogue entry for this book is available from the
British Library

Printed in Malaysia

This book is available for special discounts for bulk purchases
for sales promotions or premiums. Special editions, including
personalized covers, excerpts of existing books, and corporate
imprints, can be created in large quantities for special needs.

For more information in the USA write to Special
Markets/Premium Sales, 1745 Broadway, MD 6–2, New York,
NY 10019, or e-mail specialmarkets@randomhouse.com.

In the United Kingdom contact Kuperard publishers at the
address at the top of the page.

Cover image: Tile pattern, Abdul Raouf Hasan Khalil Museum, Jeddah.
Travel Ink/Stephen Coyne
Images on pages 72 © Hariadhi, and 87 © Ali Mansuri

About the Author

NICOLAS BUCHELE grew up in Hamburg and was educated at University College London, where he graduated with first-class honors in English Language and Literature. He left Europe in 1997 to work as a journalist in Asia. In 2003–04, he was chief sub-editor at *Arab News* in Jeddah, Saudi Arabia. He has published articles on subjects ranging from Henry James' late novels to car launches in Lebanon. He now lives in Bangkok, Thailand, where he works for Korea's largest-circulation newspaper, the *Chosun Ilbo*.

The Culture Smart! series is continuing to expand.
For further information and latest titles visit
www.culturesmartguides.com

The publishers would like to thank **CultureSmart!**Consulting for its help in researching and developing the concept for this series.

CultureSmart!Consulting creates tailor-made seminars and consultancy programs to meet a wide range of corporate, public-sector, and individual needs. Whether delivering courses on multicultural team building in the USA, preparing Chinese engineers for a posting in Europe, training call-center staff in India, or raising the awareness of police forces to the needs of diverse ethnic communities, we provide essential, practical, and powerful skills worldwide to an increasingly international workforce.

For details, visit www.culturesmartconsulting.com

CultureSmart!Consulting and **CultureSmart!** guides have both contributed to and featured regularly in the weekly travel program "Fast Track" on BBC World TV.

contents

contents

Map of Saudi Arabia

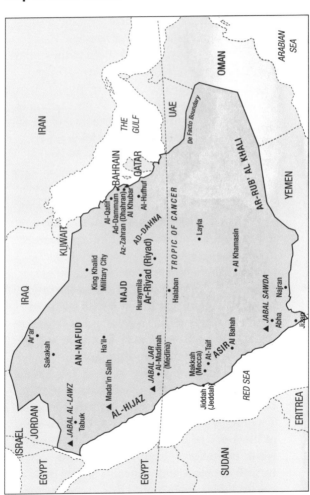

introduction

"There is no such thing as society," Margaret Thatcher famously said. "There are individual men and women and there are families." As nonsensical as this might have been in the context of Britain, it is true of Saudi Arabia—perhaps with the added proviso, "There are tribes."

It would be hard to think of another nation of 22 million so singularly free of the myriad social interconnections Westerners take for granted: neighborliness; public space; debate about the ephemera of pop culture, the pretensions of high culture, and the political issues of the day; and a media representing the full spectrum of opinion.

Yet to the outside world at least, the Kingdom of Saudi Arabia presents a uniform appearance: the traditional robes of the men and the black overgarments and veils of the women, at first glance, make the former difficult and the latter sometimes impossible to distinguish from one another; and the official religion pervading every aspect of people's lives can make it seem as if all Saudis have everything in common.

That is only the greatest of the paradoxes of Saudi Arabia, a country where stark opposites coexist without ever resolving themselves into a synthesis. "This people," wrote T. E. Lawrence of the Arabs he lived among, "was black and white, not only in vision, but by inmost furnishing; black and white not merely in clarity, but in apposition. Their thoughts were at ease only in extremes. They inhabited superlatives by choice."

Divided by region, creed, and background but united in Islam, insular yet forever traveling abroad, and living with a foreign contingent that makes up nearly one-fifth of the population: the list goes on. So what do Saudis have in common beyond their national dress? Perhaps the key characteristic is that Saudis are intensely private people. Getting to know them can be a challenge—their reticence is often masked by loud voices and what can seem an arrogant attitude—but it is a challenge worth taking up. Those who make the effort will encounter charismatic people capable of enormous charm, with great storytelling verve, and a sharp sense of humor that thrives on exaggeration. They will also encounter enormously gracious hosts.

In his own home or company, every Saudi is king. Many Saudi men have a regal demeanor, reflecting the unchallenged supremacy they enjoy within their own realm. Perhaps that is why they need to claim as much separate space as possible.

Saudi Arabia is a young nation. People under twenty-five make up as much as two-thirds of the population, and Riyadh will be the peninsula's first megacity by about 2020. For anyone interested in how a society in transition adjusts, by trial and frequent error, to new realities, it is a fascinating place to visit.

Key Facts

Official Name	Kingdom of Saudi Arabia (Al-Mamlaka al-Arabiya as-Saudiya)	Member of Arab League and Gulf Cooperation Council
Capital City	Riyadh	
Main Cities	Jeddah, Dammam, al-Khobar	
Population	27,601,038 (2007 est.), of whom 5.6 m are foreigners	Annual population growth rate 2.06%
Ethnic Makeup	Arab 90%, Afro-Asian 10%	
Age Structure	0–14 years: 38.2% 15–64 years: 59.4% 65 years and over: 2.4%	
Area	864,869 square miles (2,240,000 sq. km)	
Geography	Middle East, bordering the Persian Gulf and the Red Sea, north of Yemen	Four regions: Hijaz, Najd, Eastern Province, South
Terrain	Mostly sandy desert. Rugged mountains along the west coast give way to a central plateau; the east is rocky or sandy lowland. The huge sandy desert to the south is hostile to life.	
Climate	Desert climate, with hot days and cold nights; hot and humid on the coast	
Natural Resources	Petroleum, natural gas, iron ore, gold, copper	
Currency	Saudi riyal (SAR) US $1 = SAR 3.75	

Language	Arabic	English is widely understood. The labor communities have their own languages.
Religion	Sunni Islam, Wahhabi	The religious establishment, the *ulema*, is headed by the Grand Mufti.
Minority Faiths	Shia Islam; Christianity and Hinduism among expatriates	
Government	Absolute monarchy	The king is head of state and cabinet; an appointed *Shura* council advises; partial local elections, men only
Media	Government-controlled; satellite access to pan-Arab and international channels	Newspapers include mass-circulation *Okaz* and *Al-Watan* (in Arabic); *Arab News* and *Saudi Gazette* (in English)
Electricity	220 volts, 50 Hz	Two- or three-prong plugs, depending on age of building
DVD	Region 2; 0 widely available	
Internet	ADSL available	Heavily censored
Telephone	The country code is 966.	To call abroad, dial 00 followed by country code
Time Zone	GMT + 3 hours	

chapter one

LAND & PEOPLE

GEOGRAPHY

Saudi Arabia is a desert country about one-fifth the size of the United States, covering some 864,869 square miles (2,240,000 sq. km) of overwhelmingly arid land. And while the landscape can look much the same across the kingdom, the features that stand out do so spectacularly.

Only about 37 miles (60 km) south of the Red Sea port of Jeddah, an escarpment suddenly rises sheer some 1,640 feet (500 m) out of the flat land, and from there the mountains, including the 10,827-foot (3,300-m) Jabal Sawda, stretch ruggedly all the way into Yemen in the south.

The central rocky plateau of the Najd with the capital Riyadh is traversed by a number of wadis, or dry river beds, and isolated by three great deserts from north, east, and south. In the north, the An Nafud covers about 21,236 square miles (55,000 sq. km) at an elevation of some 3,280 feet (1,000 m), mostly with longitudinal dunes scores of miles long, as much as 295 feet (90 m) high and separated by valleys as much as 10 miles (16 km) wide, given a reddish tinge at sundown by the iron ore in the sand. To the east runs the Ad Dahna, a narrow band of sand mountains also known as the River of Sand.

To the south of the Najd lies the mother of all deserts, the Rub al-Khali or Empty Quarter, which covers more than 212,356 square miles (550,000 sq. km) of wandering dunes at higher elevations and sandy flatlands and salt flats lower down. In its far southeast are the fabled quicksands said to have swallowed whole caravans. Most of it is totally without water and uninhabited—hence the name—except for a handful of wandering Bedouin and a minimal number of plant and animal species.

To the east of the Ad Dahna lies al-Hasa, the country's largest oasis, which in fact consists of two neighboring oases including the town of al-Hofuf. It is on these fertile islands in the desert that the best of the kingdom's dates are grown.

Saudi Arabia is bordered by Yemen and Oman in the south, the Red Sea in the west, Jordan and

Iraq in the north, and Kuwait, the Persian Gulf, Qatar, and the United Arab Emirates (UAE) in the east. Across a causeway in the Gulf lies the island kingdom of Bahrain, which offers many Saudis a little weekend respite from the restrictions of their own country.

CLIMATE

Most of the country has a desert climate, which means extreme dry heat during the day and abrupt temperature drops at night. In the Najd, temperatures rise commonly to 113°F (45°C) and can go as high as 129.2°F (54°C). This contrasts with the coastal areas of the Red Sea and the Persian Gulf, where the temperature only rises above 100.4°F (38°C) in the summer but humidity is usually more than 85 percent and often 100 percent. The winter is brief, seeing a few drops of rain on the coast and even some rare snowfalls in the interior. Asir in the deep south experiences Indian Ocean monsoons, usually between October and March.

Overall, rainfall is low and erratic: it may consist of one or two torrential downpours for the entire year that flood the wadis and then rapidly disappear into the soil. While average rainfall is 3.937 inches (100 mm) per year, whole regions may not see any rain at all for several years. For much of the country, water comes from huge desalination plants on the coast or from deep wells in the interior that are forever in danger of drying up.

POPULATION

Due to the nature of the terrain and the erratic ways of government, all population figures are rough estimates, in some areas arrived at simply by over-flying the territory. According to the latest estimates (2007), there were some 27.6 million people living in the kingdom, of whom about 5.6 million, or nearly one-fifth, were foreigners. One million each are estimated to come from India and Egypt, and they also include people as diverse as Filipinos, Americans, Sri Lankans, and Somalis. This leads to the paradoxical situation in which one of the world's most closed societies has one of the world's highest percentages of "aliens" living in its midst—the percentage is probably higher than the official figures since many of the foreigners there are no longer (or never were) legal residents.

Saudis themselves may at first glance seem an extraordinarily uniform people: the white *thobe* or ankle-length robe worn by men, topped by a checkered *keffiyeh* or *ghutra*, and the all-over black of the women's *abaya* and *hijab* make the men difficult and the women sometimes impossible to distinguish. Yet in reality they are very diverse. Essentially, the kingdom consists of four distinct regions and populations. Each region has some nomadic and seminomadic elements: as recently as 1950, at least half the population were nomads. Tribal identities remain hugely important.

The Eastern Province, where the oil wealth is concentrated, has a substantial Shia population with cultural links to Iran, Bahrain, and other places in the Gulf region, as well as a component of Indian, Yemeni, and black African origins.

Asir in the south is in fact more closely linked to Yemen than to Saudi Arabia, both by population and its mountainous geography: this is the home of the one-million-strong Al-Ghamdi tribe whose members played a key role in the 9/11 bombings and terrorist attacks targeting the Saudi state. Asir is also home to the Flower Men, a small tribe of non-Muslims surviving in the mountains, who adorn their headbands with sprigs of wild flowers and cultivate perfume.

The Najd in the center is divided into three regions, with town centers that were quasi-independent city-states until the early twentieth century, some bitterly opposed to the ruling clan. Until development began in the 1960s, the Najd was relatively isolated, but its towns had populations linked to the Gulf, the Hijaz, and Africa.

The Hijaz on the west coast, home to the holy sites of Islam, was historically tied into the Ottoman bureaucratic system. The populations of Mecca, Medina, and Jeddah have for centuries been infused by descendants of foreign Muslims who came for the pilgrimage and stayed.

Mecca has substantial communities of Indian and Indonesian origin, and Jeddah has descendants of Persians and Hadramis (from Hadramaut or Aden in Yemen), as well as Africans and people from other parts of the Arabic-speaking world. Jeddah was the kingdom's unrivaled commercial center until the 1960s, and in all the Hijaz towns, merchant families still form a powerful, liberal elite.

What most Saudis do have in common, perhaps, is a certain reticence in dealing with strangers—and indeed with each other: mutual regional prejudices run deep, and many Saudis declare themselves to be something else (such as Yemeni or Jordanian) due to their tribal affiliations or ethnic origins. They also, down to the poorest farmers, share a great personal pride and an upright, almost regal bearing.

A BRIEF HISTORY
Pre-Islamic Period

Arabs have from time immemorial been herders, traders, and raiders. Civilization developed in southern Arabia by about 1000 BCE. Small

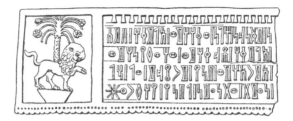

kingdoms or city-states—the best known is probably Saba, or Sheba in the Old Testament—were scattered across the land. The Romans called Yemen "Arabia Felix" (happy Arabia) because of its prosperity. Outside the coastal areas and a few centers in the Hijaz associated with the caravan trade, the harsh climate and desert limited agriculture and made the land difficult of access. The population in the hinterland probably subsisted on a combination of oasis gardening and herding, and most people were nomadic or seminomadic.

Cities that could service the camel caravans moving across the desert flourished. The most prosperous of these—Petra in Jordan and Palmyra in Syria—were close to the Mediterranean region, but small caravan cities developed on the Arabian peninsula as well. The most important was Mecca.

Some Arabs, particularly in the Hijaz, held religious beliefs that recognized multiple gods and rituals for worshiping them. They chiefly involved the sense that certain places and times of year were sacred. At those times, the near-permanent warfare between squabbling tribes, in particular, was forbidden, and various rituals were required. Foremost of these was the pilgrimage, and Mecca was the best-known pilgrimage site.

The Persians and the Romans were the great powers in the centuries before Islam, and the Arab tribes that lived near their territories were drawn into their political affairs. After 400 CE, both empires paid Arab tribes not only to protect their southern borders but also to harass the borders of their enemies. The time before Islam is generally referred to as *jahiliyya*, "the time of ignorance."

Early Islamic Period
Islam got off to a rocky start. When the Prophet Mohammed first began to preach this profoundly political religion, it angered his tribe, the Quraish, who controlled the pilgrimage traffic in Mecca and were custodians of the Kaaba, which was

already the sacred shrine of a polytheistic religion and a pilgrimage destination. For Mohammed not only attacked such things as lax marriage arrangements, the treatment of women as chattels, and the killing of unwanted offspring, he also insisted there was only one God, thus potentially endangering the lucrative pilgrim traffic to the shrine.

In 615 Mohammed sent some of his followers to safety in Christian Ethiopia while he himself remained under siege in Mecca, but in 622 he fled to the town of Yatrib, some 200 miles (320 km) north of Mecca—his emigration marks the beginning of the Islamic calendar. He renamed the city *Al-Madinah al-Munawarrah*, the City of Light, now mostly known as Medina for short. There, he took to raiding caravans for income, which incensed the Meccans who serviced them and prompted them to attack him repeatedly.

By 628, Mohammed had sufficient support to establish a truce with Mecca, finally conquering the city in 630 and smashing the three hundred and sixty idols in the Kaaba. He declared the territory surrounding the shrine *haram* (forbidden) to all non-Muslims, which it remains to this day. By his death in 632, Mohammed enjoyed the loyalty of almost all the tribes of Arabia.

Mohammed's successor Abu Bakr, the first of the "rightly guided" caliphs, asked Mohammed's former secretary Zaid ibn Thabit to write down

THE PROPHET MOHAMMED

Mohammed was one of the most extraordinary men who ever lived. Born in 570 into the Quraish, the leading tribe in Mecca, he grew up illiterate and at twenty-five married Khadija, a wealthy widow fifteen years his senior who may have been his employer. Drawn to the monotheism of Christians and Jews, he withdrew to a cave to find the truth. In 610 he began to experience visitations of the angel Gabriel dictating to him the word of God; the resulting passages of masterful poetry, which he continued to produce throughout his life, were later collected from memory in the Koran— literally "recitations."

At first, Mohammed told only Khadija about his experiences, but in 613 he began to recite them publicly. Not surprisingly, his message of unity under one God was violently resisted by the pagan Meccans. Driven into exile in Medina, Mohammed proved to be a canny politician. He contracted many alliances, often, after the death of his first wife, through marriage. The most famous was with Aisha, who was seven at the time but was to become his favorite and most influential wife. Aisha is the source of many *hadiths*, the traditions of the Prophet's sayings, that form part of the wider Islamic canon.

Mohammed expected but rarely forced pagans to submit to Islam, and allowed Christians and Jews—the "People of the Book" whose own prophets are recognized by Islam—to keep their faith provided they paid a special tax.

all the Prophet's revelations still in people's memories, producing a proto-Koran. The scriptures were passed to his successor Umar and his daughter, and under Umar's successor Uthman, the same Ibn Thabit produced a standardized, "authorized" version.

In the two years until his death, Abu Bakr maintained the loyalty of the Arab tribes by force, and in the battles that followed the Prophet's death—known as the apostasy wars—he enforced Islam across the peninsula. For the next thirty years, caliphs managed the growing Islamic empire from Medina.

With the end of the apostasy wars, the Arab tribes united behind Islam and turned their attention to the Roman and Persian empires. Arab-led armies pushed rapidly through both empires and in record time established Arab control from what is now Spain to Pakistan.

However, the empire soon ceased to be controlled from Arabia, whose importance declined. After the third caliph, Uthman, was assassinated in 656, the Muslim world was split into Sunni and Shia. The first regarded themselves as "people of the Sunnah," followers of the way in which the Prophet and his followers lived. The second believed that spiritual authority was conferred through the descendants of the fourth caliph, Ali, who spent much of his time in Iraq before he was murdered in 661 in Kufa.

After Ali, the Umayyads established a hereditary line of caliphs in Damascus until they were in turn overthrown in 750 by the Abbasids, who ruled from Baghdad. By the latter part of the eighth century, a mere two centuries after the birth of the Prophet, the political importance of Arabia in the Islamic world had declined.

The Middle Ages

While Arabia became marginalized, Mecca remained the spiritual focus of Islam because it was the destination for the pilgrimage. But it lacked political importance, which lay in Medina. After the Prophet's death, Medina continued to be an administrative center and developed into an intellectual and literary one as well. In the seventh and eighth centuries, for instance, Medina became an important center for the legal discussions that would lead to the codification of Islamic law.

What is now Saudi Arabia became divided into two distinct regions. The Hijaz was variously controlled by whoever was powerful in the empire. In 1000, this was the Ismaili Fatimid dynasty, who ruled from their new capital, Cairo. In the thirteenth century, the Mamluk sultans of Egypt became the feudal overlords of the Hijaz, and in 1517 it passed to the Ottoman Empire after the Turks conquered Egypt. It also developed its cosmopolitan atmosphere due to the constant pilgrimage traffic.

The Najd, on the other hand, was more isolated and of no great importance to the imperial masters. This was chiefly due to its geographic situation; once the Muslim empire spread, pilgrims from the west

soon found more convenient routes that avoided the deserts. That division can be felt to this day.

The Saudi-Wahhabi Pact

Around 1500, an obscure clan took over some date groves in Ad Diriyah, near Riyadh, and settled there. Over time the area developed into a small town, and the clan that would become the Al-Saud came to be recognized as its leaders. And there they would be tending their date palms to this day if it hadn't been for the trials and tribulations of one Mohammed ibn Abdul Wahhab Al-Tamimi.

Born in the Najd in 1703 or thereabouts, Abdul Wahhab became angry during his religious studies about the discrepancy between the austere rituals laid down in the Koran and the way the religion was popularly practiced, especially the worship of shrines and saints he found among the Shia he encountered in Persia. Styling himself a reformer, and determined to return Islam to the sole unchallenged worship of a single God and to fight all "innovation" from music to smoking, he spent some years destroying shrines in the Najdi towns of Huraimila and Uyainah while attempting to persuade their leaders of his ideas.

When that failed, he turned his attentions to Ad Diriyah, where he had earlier encountered some support. In 1744, the local ruler Mohammed ibn Saud and Abdul Wahhab swore a holy oath to work together to establish a state run according to Islamic principles, with Abdul Wahhab in charge of religious matters and Mohammed ibn Saud taking care of the political side. The pact still holds to this day.

The First Saudi State

Galvanized by a strong religious cause, Mohammed ibn Saud started by leading armies into Najdi towns and villages to eradicate popular and Shia practices there. By 1765 his forces had established Wahhabism—and with it Al-Saud political authority—over most of the Najd. When he died in 1765, his son Abdul Aziz continued the advance.

In 1801, the Saudi-Wahhabi armies made their first mistake when they attacked and brutally sacked Karbala, the Shia city now in eastern Iraq that grew up around the tomb of Ali's son Hussein, commemoration of whose death is the key event in the Shia calendar known as Ashura. And in 1803 they moved to take control of Sunni towns in the Hijaz, destroying monuments and grave markers that were being used for prayers to Muslim saints and for votive rituals.

This naturally drew the attention of the rest of

the Islamic world, which had previously paid no great attention to what went on in the Najd. But the practices the Wahhabis suppressed in the Hijaz were important to other Muslims, the majority of whom were alarmed that shrines were being destroyed and access to the holy cities restricted. Control of the Hijaz and the holy places was of course also a potent political symbol in the Islamic world, and the Ottoman Turks, who by then dominated it, had no intention of letting the Al-Saud get away with it.

The Ottomans delegated the recapture to an ambitious client, Mohammed Ali, the governor of Egypt, who in turn handed the job in 1816 to his son Tursun; Mohammed Ali later joined him. Mecca and Medina fell almost immediately. The then-Saudi ruler Abdullah retreated to the Najd, but was pursued by an army under Mohammed Ali's other son, Ibrahim. Battered for two years by superior Egyptian personnel and arms, Ad Diriyah, and Abdullah with it, fell in 1818.

Another century was to elapse before the Al-Saud tried again.

The Second Saudi State

In the meantime, the Al-Saud dusted themselves off and picked themselves up, forming a second state on a modest scale in their old heartland by 1824, and establishing Riyadh as the Wahhabi capital in about 1830. This lasted until 1891, when they were driven out by their most implacable enemies from the Najd, the rival Wahhabi Al-Rashid dynasty of Hail.

Ibn Saud

Abdul Aziz, widely known in the West as Ibn Saud, was born in Riyadh around 1876 but fled with his family into exile in Kuwait when the Al-Rashid took over the area. By the age of twenty-five, he was ready to launch a small raiding party on Rashidi strongholds. They soon grew to two hundred men and kept growing—the exploits of his band of merry men are still a potent legend in the kingdom today.

After a number of setbacks, Ibn Saud was able to take over the Najd by 1912. This was partly possible because the Al-Saud were only a clan without tribal allegiance, so the tribes whose loyalty he bought, or forced, or won through an endless string of marriages, would not lose face by being seen to surrender to a rival tribe—and all tribes are potential rivals of all other tribes.

During the First World War, the British sought to cultivate Ibn Saud as an ally because the Al-Rashid had made the strategic mistake of maintaining their alliance with the Ottoman Empire, by then a very "sick man" on the Bosporus. They signed a protectorate treaty with Ibn Saud that netted him £5,000 a month, recognizing him as Emir of the Najd and al-Hasa. In exchange, he was to make war on the Al-Rashid.

This presented a problem. For Ibn Saud had also earlier been chosen as the leader of a band of Wahhabi fanatics known as the Ikhwan (or brothers), who were thirsty for blood, but only of non-Wahhabi Muslims or non-Muslims, and had no quarrel with the al-Rashid.

It was therefore not until 1920 that Ibn Saud was able to thunder into action, taking over all the Rashidi strongholds by 1922 with a regular army well equipped due to the British money. That doubled his territory and allowed him to renegotiate his deal with Britain so that he was free to extend his conquests further. British subsidies continued until 1924.

Britain had also cultivated Ibn Saud's old enemy, Sherif Hussein ibn Ali in the Hijaz, backing his uprising against the Turks that expelled them from Arabia. But now, from 1919 to 1925, Ibn Saud fought the Al-Sherif, finally conquering Mecca in 1926 and ending seven hundred years of corrupt but cultured and worldly Hashemite protection of the holy places. The British compensated the Al-Sherif by carving out the kingdoms of Jordan (which they rule to this day) and Iraq. In 1926, Ibn Saud had the locals declare him King of the Hijaz in an informal referendum.

The conquest of the Hijaz was achieved, however, at great human cost for the local population, whose enduring resentment of Wahhabism can in part be traced to the 1924 Taif massacre, where the Ikhwan slaughtered at least three hundred of the citizens to cries of "infidel" and "heretic." Ironically perhaps, Ibn Saud himself was to die in Taif in 1953.

The Birth of a Kingdom

Ibn Saud faced the immediate challenge of moderating the religious fanaticism that had served him well during the conquests but would not do so in the long term if he was to establish his tenuous religious and worldly authority over the conquered territories.

This meant getting rid of the Ikhwan, who made no concessions to life in the twentieth century. They objected to machines like the telegraph, as well as to the increasing presence of non-Muslim foreigners in the country. They also remained eager to force their message on whoever did not accept it, non-Wahhabi Muslims and sometimes Wahhabi Muslims alike, both within the territory and beyond its borders in Iraq, which provoked the British.

The king was finally forced to wage battle on the Ikhwan and defeated them in 1929. In 1932, he was ready to combine his two realms: he proclaimed the united Kingdom of Saudi Arabia, naming it after his own family. On the surface at least, he had achieved the impossible: uniting the feuding tribes and disparate towns of Arabia into a single nation under Islam.

The structure had one major weakness, in that its superficial homogeneity of belief and allegiance could not endure by force or faith alone: it required constant payouts to ensure the loyalty of the tribes.

The Discovery of Oil
Another stroke of luck for the new king, then, was the discovery of vast reserves of oil under what became known as the Eastern Province, the Shia-majority coastal areas east of the Najd, early in the century. Within the kingdom, oil continues to be portrayed as a reward from God for faithful adherence to Islam through the centuries of eking out a meager living from the desert. Abroad, it

attracted the attention of the most forward-looking, pragmatic, and technology-savvy global player of the time, the United States.

Ibn Saud granted the first concession to a British conglomerate in 1923, before he had even conquered the country. By the early 1940s, the extent of Saudi oil resources had become known and US petroleum companies, which bought the concessions in the 1930s after Britain inexplicably allowed them to lapse, urged Washington to assume more responsibility for them. Setting a pattern for the future, the administration of Franklin D. Roosevelt listened intently and declared in 1943 that the defense of Saudi Arabia was of vital interest to the USA. It dispatched a military mission to the kingdom; among other things, it built an airfield in Dhahran, later to become famous as a launch pad in the First Gulf War (1990–91).

In early 1945, a fateful meeting took place between Ibn Saud and Roosevelt aboard the USS *Quincy* in the Suez Canal. It cemented the Al-Saud's second great alliance, whereby they effectively handed defense and regime security over to the USA and guaranteed a steady supply of cheap oil in return. It was to prove as unbreakable for both sides as the first alliance.

A year earlier, several American oil firms had formed the Arabian American Oil Company, or Aramco for short, which was run chiefly by

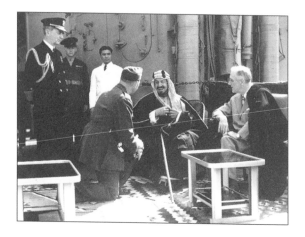

Texaco but added Standard Oil Company of New Jersey (later Exxon) and Socony-Vacuum (now Mobil Oil) for more investment cash. They had the sole concession until the 1970s, but the agreement was modified so many times that control of the oil for all intents and purposes returned to the Saudi state.

For Ibn Saud, the sudden, unstoppable spring of money, which must have looked like nothing so much as a newly struck oil fountain in the movies, was a godsend, allowing him to buy the loyalties he needed with handouts to tribal sheikhs as well as an ever-growing family of princes and princesses. The money duly trickled down to ordinary members of the tribes and other commoners and almost kept everyone in line for the next half century.

THE SUCCESSION

Ibn Saud had some sixty children. Although it was not initially set down in writing, it was understood that he would be succeeded by every one of his sons before the crown could pass on to the next generation. The Al-Saud being a hardy, long-lived family, the line of sons has by no means come to an end. But the result has been that the kingdom's rulers have got older and older while their subjects, due to the population explosion, have become younger and younger: some two-thirds of Saudis are under twenty-five, but King Abdullah was eighty-three at the time of writing, and Crown Prince Sultan a sprightly seventy-nine.

It has also meant constant infighting behind the scenes over who is next up, with various rival branches of the vast family jockeying for poll position. In 2006 King Abdullah passed a succession law that established a new body, the Allegiance Commission, exclusively made up of male heirs to Ibn Saud, which will have the job of ensuring the smooth transfer of power. The aim was to reduce uncertainty and, it is generally understood, make it possible at last for a member of the younger generation to take over after Crown Prince Sultan.

King Saud (1953–64)

When Ibn Saud died in 1953, the crown passed to his oldest surviving son, Saud. A spendthrift before he became king, he remained a spendthrift afterward: Saud paid huge sums to maintain tribal acquiescence to his rule in return for recruits to an immense palace guard, the White Army. Although the oil money had started flowing to the tune of some US $300 million a year, revenues could not match Saud's expenditures for the tribes, subsidies to various foreign groups, and his personal follies. In 1958 the riyal had to be devalued by nearly 80 percent.

All this happened, of course, at the expense of public projects, education, and the wages of the growing labor force, who were paid a pittance. In Ibn Saud's day, the privileged classes had been far less visible, and the king's own first palace was built of mud bricks; so this marked the beginning of the dual culture that is now inextricably associated with Saudi Arabia.

Dissatisfaction came not only from liberal princes but, to the alarm of the ruling family, from a small nascent middle class who were educated abroad. One result is that the Saudi regime has since done everything it can to prevent the emergence of a larger middle class that could pose a political challenge—by hobbling education and by farming professional jobs out to foreigners and opening only menial work to Saudis.

Abroad, King Saud also acted erratically, at first promoting Arab nationalism in Egypt and elsewhere and managing to annoy his country's most important ally, the United States; then, after a meeting with US President Eisenhower, performing a complete U-turn. At home, meanwhile, he kept appointing his own young, inexperienced sons—of whom he had even more than Ibn Saud—to positions of power.

He clearly had become a liability, and in 1958 senior members of the Al-Saud forced him to relinquish power to his half brother, Faisal. At first, Faisal was made prime minister under Saud, declining the kingship due to a promise he had made to his father. He resigned in 1960 but was later reinstated; in the brief interlude, Saud involved his military in an ill-advised adventure in Yemen, supporting royalist forces in the civil war there.

Saud was finally deposed by *fatwa* in 1964, fleeing to Switzerland from where he continued to embarrass his country, and Faisal took the throne.

King Faisal (1964–75)

The rule of Faisal is regarded as a golden age for the kingdom. Already as prime minister under Saud in 1962, he had set about modernizing the country, introducing a reform package that included promises to issue a constitution, establish local government, and form an independent judiciary with a supreme judicial council composed of both secular and religious members.

Faisal was also to regulate economic and commercial activities, introducing a program of austerity and sound fiscal management, and there was to be a sustained effort to develop the country's resources. Social reforms would include provisions for social security, unemployment compensation, educational scholarships, and the abolition of slavery. He also pledged to strengthen Islam and to reform the Committee for the Promotion of Virtue and Prevention of Vice, the *mutawwa* (religious police: see page 124).

Faisal's first two official acts were protective. In the first month of his rule, Khaled, a half brother, was designated crown prince, thus ensuring that the succession would not be disturbed by family power politics. Sultan, another half brother, then as now minister of defense and aviation, was charged with modernizing the army and establishing an air defense system to protect the country and its oil reserves.

In the field of education, funds to King Abdul Aziz University in Jeddah were substantially increased, and the University of Petroleum and Minerals was opened in Dhahran. Faisal also instituted education for girls (initially on a voluntary basis), against fierce resistance from the religious establishment, the *ulema*.

Yet while allying himself with the liberal, cosmopolitan merchants who were still powerful in the Hijaz and keeping the Wahhabi hard-liners in check, Faisal was no liberal himself, calling an Islamic Conference to try and affirm the Saudi state's principles against rising republican movements in the Arab world. A realist, he chose the middle ground, permitting television in 1965 over violent protests from fanatical members of his own family, but banning labor unions the same year.

Faisal also ended the long-standing problem of the Yemen civil war by reaching a ceasefire with Gamal Abdel Nasser of Egypt, who supported the republican forces. The 1967 Arab-Israeli war, which resulted in a swift, humiliating rout for Egypt and the annexation of vast Arab territories, meant Nasser could no longer afford the war in Yemen and he agreed with Faisal to end financial and military support.

The Arab Conference at Khartoum in 1967 agreed neither to recognize nor to make peace with Israel and to continue to work for the rights of the Palestinians. It was in this context that Saudi Arabia was for the first and last time openly to wield the oil weapon.

In his international dealings as well as at home, the king relied a great deal on his protégé and oil minister, Sheikh Zaki Yamani. Yamani, a Harvard-educated Hijazi and natural performer given to impeccably timed antics, became a well-known face on the international stage. (He later achieved even greater fame when he survived an abduction by the famous terrorist Carlos the Jackal.) In 1967, Yamani spoke against an oil embargo, but the West's renewed support for Israel in the 1973 Arab-Israeli war was too much for the Saudis.

Led by Saudi Arabia, the Organization of the Petroleum Exporting Countries (OPEC) imposed

a general rise in oil prices and an oil embargo on major oil consumers who were either supporters of Israel or allies of its supporters. The embargo was theoretically aimed at forcing Israel to withdraw from the occupied territories and recognize the rights of the Palestinian people.

In reality, Yamani was to travel around the world to negotiate exceptions with practically every nation this affected, from Germany to the USA—but not before the pumps had run dry and prices skyrocketed, giving them a taste of the power the Arabs could wield if they chose.

As a result, the price of crude oil tripled and Saudi Arabia in the resulting boom acquired massive revenues for spending on domestic programs. However, Faisal's failing health, overwork, and age prevented him from formulating a coherent development plan. He was assassinated on March 25, 1975, shot by a disgruntled hard-line nephew.

Sheikh Yamani remained oil minister, but with greatly reduced influence and at increasing odds with his kings and their coterie, until Fahd finally dismissed him in 1986. Today, he more or less openly leads a small elite movement for Hijazi independence and devotes himself—in what is in itself a form of rebellion—to preserving important cultural sites.

King Khaled (1975–82)

The years after Faisal were a time of cementing state control over Saudi society and, emboldened by the oil crisis, of greater engagement abroad. They were also a time of population explosion fueled by the oil boom. Khaled himself had no great interest in government, being a committed falconer who loved the desert and suffering from a heart ailment. One distinction of Khaled's rule was that Saudi Arabia, improbably, became a net exporter of wheat.

Khaled soon handed the running of the country over to his younger half brother Fahd, a gambler, playboy, and lover of the high life who was also an ambitious politician.

The rich flow of petrodollars and cautious modernization had created a false sense of peace. That was violently shattered when, on November 20, 1979, some five hundred Wahhabi fanatics invaded and seized the Grand Mosque in Mecca. Their leader, Juhaiman Al-Otaibi, was from one of the leading families of the Najd, whose family members had been among the foremost of the Ikhwan. Juhaiman said his justification was that the Al-Saud had lost their legitimacy through "corruption, ostentation, and mindless imitation of the West."

Juhaiman's party included women as well as men, other peninsular Arabs, and a few Egyptians. A score of the dissidents were unemployed graduates of the kingdom's seminary in Medina. They had provisions for the siege they expected as well as extensive supplies of arms.

The Saudi leadership was initially paralyzed. Because of the holiness of the Grand Mosque, it comes under a special injunction in Islam: it is forbidden to shed blood there or to deface or pollute it in any way. Before any military move could be authorized, the *ulema* (religious establishment) had to issue a dispensation to allow the bearing of arms in a holy place. When the religious issues had been solved, logistical problems bogged down the efforts of the military and the National Guard for several days. Finally, two weeks later, the military succeeded in routing the dissidents. All the surviving men were beheaded in the squares of four cities.

Then, just two weeks later, Shia riots broke out in al-Qatif in the Eastern Province, emboldened by the triumphant return to Iran of Ayatollah Khomeini earlier that year. Many of the rioters bore posters with Khomeini's picture. Up to twenty thousand National Guard troops were immediately moved into the Eastern Province. Several demonstrators were killed and hundreds reportedly arrested.

The Al-Saud's response was characteristic: to appease the Wahhabi hard-liners, they moved to "strengthen" Islam by tightening religious restrictions on ordinary Saudis and handed more powers to the *ulema*; to appease the Shia, who dominated the vital, oil-rich Eastern Province, they announced development projects—more money—in the Shia heartland of al-Qatif and al-Hofuf.

The final year of Khaled's reign also saw the birth of the first Saudi peace plan for Palestine, which partly aims to sideline Iranian influence and stresses the need for a comprehensive settlement—the creation of a Palestinian state and Arab recognition of Israel's right to exist in exchange for Israeli withdrawal from the West Bank and the Gaza Strip.

Fahd's other foreign policy initiatives often aimed to counter Iranian influence. But they also included the formation of the Gulf Cooperation Council (GCC) and helping avert an escalation in the Morocco–Algeria conflict in 1981.

King Khaled died in 1982.

King Fahd (1982–2005)

Fahd was the oldest of the so-called Sudairi Seven, the sons of Ibn Saud by his wife Hussah bint Ahmad Al-Sudairi. The seven were the most powerful bloc within the clan and served in leading positions under Fahd, from Interior Minister Prince Naif to Riyadh Governor Prince Salman.

Despite that, Fahd named his half brother Abdullah, who had been close to Faisal and headed the National Guard (which effectively became his private army), as crown prince. One of the first problems faced by the new king was a 20 percent drop in oil revenues, as a result of a world oil surplus that had developed by 1982. But despite the fall in revenues, until the oil price crash of 1986 Saudi Arabia made no significant changes in the oil policies it had followed since the oil boom years— apparently against the advice of Sheikh Yamani.

Fahd maintained his own lavish lifestyle—he had a yacht with two swimming pools, a portable garden, and later a battery of Stinger missiles— but styled himself "Custodian of the two Holy Mosques" and stepped up enforcement of the segregation of the sexes and censorship at home in an attempt to regain the Islamic high ground.

In 1987, rioting by Shia pilgrims in Mecca led to four hundred deaths and was the straw that broke the kingdom's diplomatic relations with Iran. Fahd inevitably supported Saddam Hussein's Iraq in the war against Iran. But he relied heavily on the alliance with the USA, and in the First Gulf War, after Iraq invaded Kuwait, permitted US forces to launch their attack on Iraq from Saudi soil—a decision that was to strengthen support for domestic terrorism in the twilight years of his reign.

In 1992, under international pressure to move toward democracy, Fahd finally declared a Basic Law, promised since 1962, that proved an all-round disappointment and did little more than enshrine in writing the rule of the offspring of Ibn Saud. A year later, he also set up an appointed advisory council, the *Shura*, in an attempt to silence calls for greater public participation; this was successively enlarged to 150 members by 2005.

In 1995, Fahd suffered a stroke that left him unable to continue in government. His powerful Sudairi brothers did not allow him to abdicate; instead, Abdullah became the de facto ruler but Fahd was still wheeled into meetings for Saudi TV and was occasionally reported to have made "speeches," notably an address in 2003 vowing to eradicate terrorism "with an iron fist." He died in 2005.

King Abdullah (2005–)

Abdullah for many years enjoyed a reputation as a reformer in the international press, a misunderstanding that equated his relatively modest, pious lifestyle and old-fashioned belief in talking opponents out of it with sympathy with the liberal cause. In fact, Abdullah had learned a measure of realism from Faisal and probably courted the support of the liberal branch of the Al-Saud (which includes Faisal's son Turki al-Faisal) to hold out against the Sudairi Seven.

Odd lapses, such as Abdullah's attribution of terrorist attacks in the kingdom to "Zionists," were

overlooked, but his true colors became more evident when one of his first moves on the throne, despite constantly stressing "moderation" as an Islamic virtue, was to appoint a religious hard-liner as education minister. Limited local elections that allowed only men to vote, which he had instigated as regent under Fahd, also proved a fig leaf and mostly handed victory to Wahhabi hard-liners.

Then oil prices skyrocketed in the mid-2000s, and the renewed flood of petrodollars meant that the promised reforms could be safely put aside. Internationally, Abdullah has been an active proponent of the 2001 Saudi Peace Plan, drawn up in Fahd's day to settle the Israeli-Palestinian conflict. The kingdom's repeated attempts to join the World Trade Organization finally paid off in 2005.

Domestically, Abdullah faces the challenges of massive unemployment, an exploding population, a growing gap between rich and poor, discontent, rapid urbanization, and an information revolution that has completely bypassed rulers who grew up riding through the desert by their father's side.

TERRORISM

The modern ideology of Islamism is often traced to the work of Sayyid Qutb, an extremist member of *al-Jamaah al-Islamiya*, the Muslim Brotherhood of Egypt, who was executed and thus for many turned into a martyr by Nasser. While Islam forbids warfare under the covenant of those living in Muslim lands, Qutb hit on the ingenious solution of declaring that secular, Nasserite Egypt was in fact ruled by *jahiliyya*, or pre-Islamic ignorance, which justified jihad understood as violent struggle.

Due to persecution in Egypt, many Muslim Brothers ended up in Saudi Arabia, often as teachers, where they came under the influence of radical Wahhabism and in turn infused it with their own version of radical Islam: the mixture was to prove literally explosive.

But terrorism is a protean phenomenon: it also feeds off ancient tribal resentment, the settling of old scores, social inequality, and sheer bloodlust. Al-Qaeda is largely unknowable because, if such an entity exists at all, it is at most a loose network of independent cells; what is certain is that the first-generation leaders of Islamist terrorism acquired their taste for ruthless tactics in the struggle against the Soviet occupation of Afghanistan, which many Saudis went to join.

Once that was over, they cast around for another enemy, hitting inevitably on America. Support came from disparate groups: Wahhabi hard-liners who relentlessly preached hatred of America; remnants of the 1979 occupation of the Grand Mosque; the Al-Ghamdi tribe of Asir, who resented Saudi rule over their land, and disaffected youngsters in the cities.

On September 11, 2001, fifteen of the nineteen hijackers who flew planes into the World Trade Center in New York and the Pentagon in Washington were Saudis, and many of them were Al-Ghamdi. For some time, it seems, their spiritual leader, Osama bin Laden, scion of a wealthy Jeddah family with tribal roots in Yemen, intended to spare his home country, for various complex reasons to do with financial support and the country's state ideology.

But on May 12, 2003, terrorism came home when militants drove trucks laden with explosives right into the most populated parts of three residential compounds in Riyadh and blew them up, killing thirty-five people and wounding some one hundred and fifty. The recent movie *The Kingdom* is a fanciful account of the event.

Saudi Arabia waged a relentless campaign against terrorists at home and eventually managed to kill or arrest most of their leaders in the kingdom. The ongoing civil war in Iraq also seems to have acted as a poultice, drawing Saudi militants abroad with the promise of cash and jihadist glory.

THE POLITICAL SYSTEM

The great age of ideologies was the perfect time for Ibn Saud to establish the state his ancestor had promised Mohammed ibn Abdul Wahhab. Without written constitution or express declaration, Saudi Arabia became a centralized state that took Islam as its official ideology, much in the way that communism was adopted as the ruling ideology of the Soviet Union.

The structure is based on the Caliphate believed to have existed right after the Prophet's death: its pillars are veneration of the ruler, *shura* (consultancy)—as personified in the 150-member appointed *Shura* council—and a religious authority in the form of the *ulema* led by the Grand Mufti.

Because there is no separation of religion and state, the political role of the *ulema* is second in importance only to the ruling family; they form a kind of politburo of Islam. Even if the *ulema* are engaged in a permanent tug-of-war with the worldly tendencies of the Al-Saud, both sides need the arrangement because it allows them to couch their power play in the ineffable language of religion and to enforce decisions without popular sanction.

The leading *ulema*, honoring the original Saudi-Wahhabi pact, are still the descendants of Mohammed ibn Abdul Wahhab, the Al-Asheikh family. And so the two clans continue locked in an embrace that will allow neither to triumph at the expense of the other; if one goes, so will the other.

The legal system is based on Shariah law, which in the kingdom relies on the Hanbali *fiqh*, one of the four legal schools in Islam. There are several hundred Shariah courts as well as some special tribunals established by decree, such as the Labor Court, and two appeals courts in Riyadh and Mecca. The minister of justice, appointed by the king from among the most senior *ulema*, is the de facto chief justice.

THE ECONOMY

Saudi Arabia is the world's largest oil exporter, with one-quarter of the world's proven oil reserves, mostly in the Eastern Province, home to the giant government-owned oil corporation Saudi Aramco that functions almost as a state within a state. It produces 9.48 million barrels per day and exports 8.554 million bbl of that. Oil accounts for 75 percent of budget earnings, at least 45 percent of GDP and 90 percent of exports. Today, China and Japan are its biggest customers, and the kingdom is diversifying markets, especially in Asia.

Every time the government begins to take seriously warnings that the oil will dry up and it must diversify the economy, another vast deposit is discovered. The kingdom also has huge reserves of natural gas, producing some 7 billion cubic feet (198,217,926 cubic meters) a day.

However, the government is promoting private-sector and foreign participation in the power generation, telecom, natural gas, and the burgeoning petrochemical industries. It has also recently boosted spending

on job training, infrastructure development, and government salaries. Like many developing countries, it has also announced plans to establish six "economic cities" in different regions to promote development and diversification.

Saudi Arabia is also a nation of shopkeepers, many of them running small import-export and trading businesses. Some 3.3 percent of GDP comes from agriculture, mostly livestock and the cultivation of wheat, barley, tomatoes, melons, dates, and citrus fruit.

The labor force is some 7.1 million. Given that there are some 5.6 million foreigners in the country, that probably means that the Saudi labor force is around 2 to 3 million strong. The level of unemployment is estimated at anywhere between 13 and 25 percent.

A GLOBAL AND REGIONAL POWER

The kingdom is becoming ever more active in foreign policy, both overtly and behind the scenes, and is beginning to claim a place commensurate with its vast oil wealth and control of a key resource. It is perhaps also realizing that the isolationism of the past—its "special status"—is no longer tenable and it must engage with the world.

One facet of asserting its regional influence has been its pursuit of the peace plan for Palestine. (Foreign Minister Saud al-Faisal attended the

Palestinian–Israeli summit at Annapolis in November 2007.) Another is what appears to be an attempt to counter Iranian influence in Iraq with support for Sunni factions there—though at the same time the Saudis in a high-level meeting with the Iranian leadership have vowed to head off sectarian conflict in Iraq.

In continuing to oblige the United States through the supply of cheap oil, massive arms purchases, and other support, the kingdom has also ensured for itself both wider influence and a status of international respectability—it is, for instance, a member of the UN Commission for Human Rights—that critics say it has yet to earn.

Refusing to be drawn about Israeli and US threats to bomb Iranian nuclear reactors, King Abdullah in late 2007 told the BBC's John Simpson, "I have not spoken about some subjects because I did not want either to be dishonest or evasive with you." "Maybe," Simpson concluded, "he wanted to demonstrate how independent-minded Saudi Arabia has become during his rule." The jury is out on that conclusion.

chapter two

VALUES & ATTITUDES

ISLAM

Saudi Arabia is unimaginable without Islam, the main source of its legitimacy. Most Saudis are pious and discharge their formal religious duties punctiliously. Shops and government offices shut and many people drop whatever they are doing for the five-times-daily prayer. It is not uncommon to see people abruptly stop their car at the nearest mosque when the call to prayer sounds or even pray in the street outside—though it is equally common to see them blithely driving on. No restaurants are open in daylight hours during the fasting month of Ramadan.

The kingdom's western Hijaz region is home to Mecca (the birthplace of the Prophet Mohammed) and its sister city, Medina, which form the destination for the great annual pilgrimage or Hajj. For that reason, Saudis like to refer to their country as the home or cradle of Islam, even though no such political entity existed at the time of the Prophet. The uniform traditional Saudi garb is frequently called "Islamic dress." There is a widespread notion among Saudis that they are the "true" Muslims, a perception that sometimes offends (and sometimes awes) Muslims from other countries.

If Saudi commentators endlessly debate the kingdom's "special status," it is mainly because of its custodianship of the holiest places of Islam. Almost everything in Saudi Arabia, from public debate to art and architecture, is predicated on, and circumscribed by, Islam.

THE FIVE PILLARS OF ISLAM

The *shahada*, or creed. It simply consists of the words, "There is no God except God and Mohammed is his Prophet." By reciting it, a person is considered a Muslim.

Prayer five times a day.

Fasting during the month of Ramadan.

Zakat, or almsgiving.

The Hajj, or pilgrimage to Mecca, which every able-bodied Muslim should perform at least once in their lifetime.

Religion and State

A literal, back-to-basics form of Sunni Islam known as Wahhabism is both the national religion and the state ideology of Saudi Arabia. It is named after Mohammed ibn Abdul Wahhab (1703–92 CE), the religious reformer born in the Saudi heartland of the Najd, who formed the power-sharing alliance with the House of Saud that lasts to this day. In his quest for the pure Islam he believed was embodied by the earliest converts to the faith, the *as-salaf as-salihin*, Abdul Wahhab condemned any "innovations" he saw in the decadent Ottoman Empire and among the Sufis and the Shia, especially the veneration of saints and worship at shrines, but also music and smoking.

One of its most striking features, of course, is the strict segregation of men and women enforced across the kingdom, especially in the Najd and its capital Riyadh. More broadly, it stresses the "oneness" of God, or *tawhid*—that there is no other god and nothing approaching divinity can be ascribed to anyone or anything else—and "closing the doors" (and the doors to the doors) to transgression. Hard-line Wahhabis frown even on excessive veneration of the person of Mohammed, to whom, Muslims believe, the final word of God was revealed in the Koran.

All the country's leading mosques are Wahhabi in outlook, as their austere architecture testifies, and the activities of its religious scholars can sometimes seem like a frantic search in an overcrowded field for whatever else might be *haram*, or forbidden. The language and legalistic terminology of Wahhabi belief, which is heavy on the denunciation of sins, heretics, and infidels, thunders weekly in Friday sermons from the country's two holiest mosques—the Grand Mosque in Mecca and the Prophet's Mosque in Medina—whose imams are key figures in the Saudi state's religious establishment.

To say that there is no separation between state and religion is an understatement: they are inextricably enmeshed. Fahd was the first king to assume the title "Custodian of the two Holy Mosques," and the present king, Abdullah, has inherited it. Because Wahhabism has been instrumental in Saudi nation building, it is officially the sole variety of Islam practiced in the kingdom. It is intensively taught in its schools and relentlessly propagated in books, sermons, and on TV in the country; official Saudi charities lavishly sponsor its spread around the globe. The *mutawwa* enforce Wahhabi practice where they can.

The kingdom is governed by Shariah, or Islamic law. Alcohol is prohibited, men can have four wives, and the sentence for a number of crimes including murder, sodomy, and witchcraft is death by public beheading, though a murder can be redeemed by the payment of "blood money" (*diyah*) to the victim's family. In 2006, at least thirty-seven people were publicly executed by the sword, and the previous year the number was eighty-five, almost invariably foreigners from poor countries. The punishment for theft is the amputation of a hand, though this is rarely enforced.

Wahhabism can therefore seem all-pervasive to outsiders. Yet the further away from the Wahhabi heartland, the more likely Saudis are to remain Muslims of other stripes. In the Eastern Province, a Shia majority quietly practice their faith under threat of harassment. Ironically, in the Hijaz, the very region where the two holy mosques stand, most locals privately adhere to more tolerant forms of Sunni Islam, and this is reflected in the comparatively relaxed attitude they take to the mingling of the sexes and other official taboos.

No other religions are tolerated in Saudi Arabia. It was the interior minister Prince Naif who said in 2002, "There have never been, and there will never be, churches in the Kingdom of Saudi Arabia." The same is of course true for Buddhist or Hindu temples, to say nothing of synagogues. In Islam, followers of the revealed regional religions Mohammed knew of—Judaism and Christianity—are in theory respected as "People of the Book," that is, of revelations on the road to the final word of the Koran, but the rest are just pagans. Under Shariah law, the punishment for apostasy—abandoning the faith—is death, and proselytizing Christians have been imprisoned. Bibles can in theory be confiscated, though this rarely happens unless they are imported in numbers.

Bewilderingly, the greatest challenge to the official religion comes not from liberal Islam or secularism but from an even more hard-line ideology that is gaining ground, especially among increasingly disenfranchised young people in Saudi cities. To Western visitors, the difference between the extremist theocratic state favored by Osama bin Laden and his ilk can seem little different from the already existing Wahhabi state, but to the Saudi establishment it is a matter of life and death.

TRIBAL LOYALTIES

Saudi Arabia is essentially a tribal society. When the Al-Saud clan carved out their kingdom from Yemen to Jordan, they did so by conquest and by buying off the Bedouin chieftains who ruled over their tribes across the land, who would in turn pass on the handouts to members of their tribe in the form of allowances.

To this day, the loyalties of most Saudis are locked in concentric circles, the innermost circle being the family, followed by the tribe, then friends, then the nation, then the Muslim *ummah* (community or nation), and finally everyone else. And these loyalties can take precedence over other commitments such as contractual obligations or political affiliations. Members of a tribe, even when they have spent almost their entire lives abroad, will remain in close touch with the goings-on at home, to the point of knowing what day a party is being thrown at "headquarters."

The Hijaz, for instance, was for centuries governed by the Hashemites, now the rulers of Jordan. Members of the tribe in the Hijaz, who carry the surname-cum-honorific Al-Sherif, can be heard to deny they are Saudis even when it turns out they have a Saudi passport, because their higher loyalty is to the tribe. In Asir in the south live the Al-Ghamdi, who, as mentioned previously, achieved notoriety when it was revealed that many of the 9/11 attackers on New York and Washington and prominent Al-Qaeda leaders in the kingdom belonged to the tribe.

On Saudi TV, meetings of the king with tribal leaders are often broadcast live, at baffling length to outsiders (and to the looped strains of Beethoven's Fifth), due to the importance of visibly affirming their loyalty to the ruling family. Especially in the wake of events that could be seen as divisive, tribal sheikhs are paraded before the cameras reading out statements expressing their commitment to king and country.

There are also many Saudis whose families settled there from other parts of the Muslim world and were given citizenship in the early days of the kingdom. With surnames like Al-Hindi (meaning from India) or Al-Maghribi (from the Maghrib, or North Africa), they often complain of discrimination because they are seen as "lesser" Saudis by those whose surnames identify them as belonging to one of the Arab tribes of the heartland. Among tribal Saudis, marriage between cousins remains common.

Yet despite their intense pride in their tribal heritage, urban Saudis also like to make fun of the Bedouin, the kingdom's yokels. In fact, in the country's fast-growing cities, these structures are gradually loosening, and local or class affiliations are just beginning to take the place of tribal loyalties.

HONOR

Honor is of central importance to men throughout the Arab world. To Saudis, it is vital to behave honorably in their daily dealings: not to steal, to be a generous host, a good Muslim, a good provider, and so forth. There is still very little crime in Saudi Arabia—for example, a forgotten item will probably still be where you left it even if you return for it days later.

By the same token, injuries to a man's honor are considered very serious. Many Arab men are forever bristling at some real or imagined slight, and a feud can last for decades even within the tribal network. So-called honor killings of women caught in adultery—attempts to expunge the dishonor they have supposedly brought on their family—are not unheard-of in rural Saudi Arabia. Needless to say, casting aspersions on a man's parentage or the conduct of his mother is particularly hurtful.

Respect and its outward expression are crucial, from young to old, from guest to host, from business partner to business partner. In conflicts, there is a great deal of shouting and reference to one's injured honor—often as a way to gain leverage in a losing argument—and face must be saved at all cost.

When the husband of the TV presenter Rania Al-Baz made worldwide headlines in 2004 by beating his wife half to death—and thereby brought dishonor on the entire nation—many Saudis pointed out on Internet discussion boards that he was not a "true" Saudi: his surname, Al-Falatta, suggests North African origins.

FAMILY AND PRIVACY

Most Saudi homes are shut off from the outside by high walls or, in the city centers, boarded-up apartment windows; this is a visible manifestation of the centrality of the family in the life of its people, and the exclusion of much else. Apart from Islam, the family is the central focus of Saudi life. Often several generations live under one roof, although younger Saudis increasingly hope for a family home of their own—one factor that makes marriage prohibitively expensive for young people.

Much of Saudi social interaction takes place within the family. The limited entertainment available is overwhelmingly geared to families: amusement parks are restricted to them, and restaurants have a "family section" where they can eat together hidden from the intrusive glances of outsiders.

But even where there are other options, Saudis prefer to enjoy themselves within the family and behind walls or partitions. Where cities elsewhere in the Arab world have vibrant if almost exclusively male centers where the men talk, play backgammon, and smoke their *shisha*, or hookah, in Saudi Arabia they have a forlorn, windswept aspect except in areas where foreigners from elsewhere in the Middle East congregate.

This near-complete lack of social space is partly explained by the fact that Saudis are intensely private people. They have many reasons for this, not least the authorities' constant intrusion into how they are supposed to live their lives.

There is some debate over whether there is an absolute right to privacy in Islam, but it is certainly highly prized in the kingdom. And if Saudis are initially suspicious of strangers, they can also be suspicious of each other: it is not rare for Saudis to suspect a neighbor, colleague, or relative of plotting against them. Lack of real interaction is fertile ground for rumor. On the plus side, the family home is sacrosanct, and no one, not even the *mutawwa*, can simply barge in. And no one would dream of intruding into a visitor's private space.

The Family Home

On Jeddah's Corniche stands a lavish villa in the Greco-Roman style whose owners must have reckoned without the multistory condos and hotels that have shot up on either side of it. Now, the villa crouches incongruously within a giant steel and canvas hangar that protects the residents from being spied on by their neighbors.

THE POSITION OF WOMEN

As far as it's possible to generalize, most Saudis believe men and women have very different roles in life, and many—but by no means all—feel it would be unwise to mix them. Wahhabi orthodoxy, however, puts the most radical construction imaginable on the rights and position of women. Once, Islam led the way in, for example, giving women property rights, but like so many of the great achievements of the Arab world, that is in the past.

Nor is it helpful to discuss what "Islam" does or does not permit—the debate rages incessantly throughout the Muslim world. All that can be said is that in the daily reality of the kingdom, women's freedom is severely restricted, and not just to Western eyes. Women are not allowed to drive a car; they are in principle not free to move about outside the home unaccompanied by a male guardian, or *mahram*, or to represent themselves in their legal or business dealings; they are required to cover their body and most of their face in public.

The origin of these restrictions is a combination of tribal mores and the extreme zealotry that characterizes Wahhabi religious scholarship. Hard-liners justify the prohibitions on religious grounds: they see women as inherently wanton temptresses, who must be contained, for their own good, by a firm male hand. In tribal custom, it made sense at one stage to keep one's womenfolk from the acquisitive gaze of rival tribes (among some tribes in the Najd, women apparently conceal their bodies and faces even from their husbands). In any case, the two have by now become inextricably entwined.

In theory, segregation merely defines the distinct roles of men and women: men take care of business, while women rule in the home. But in reality, it is the women who lose out on many fronts, and such sway as they hold in the home depends on a strong character and the acquiescence of husbands and fathers. A man can divorce his wife, but a woman cannot divorce her husband—in exceptional circumstances, she can persuade a judge to compel the husband to divorce her.

At the same time, things are in practice by no means as shocking to Western sensibilities as they may look on paper. For example, while men can have up to four wives, it should be said that few do, partly because they are by law financially responsible for a wife and any offspring. In fact monogamy, often by choice, is far more common.

And due to the importance of kinship ties, some women rely on their own paternal relatives to act in their defense when they have problems with their husband: not to beat around the bush, their brothers may come round and rough the husband up. This hints at another complex issue: women and their honor. A man's mother, for instance, is conventionally beyond reproach. At the dark end of the spectrum, so-called honor killings still occur in rural areas, as they do in other tribal societies.

The Veil
The *hijab*, or veil, that variously covers the head, or the entire face except the eyes, or even the eyes, has become a massive political issue around the world. Privileged Saudi women called on to explain the practice abroad may claim that it is "not an issue," but the fact is that dropping it remains a potent political statement in the kingdom, even more so than donning it can be in the West.

When a group of Saudi businesswomen took off their *abayas* and mingled freely with the men at a government-sponsored business conference in Jeddah in 2004, they were met with a barrage of condemnation from the *ulema*, with one imam of the Grand Mosque holding up "indifference to the veil" as one reason for a drought the kingdom was experiencing. Elsewhere, however, radical Islamist women are heard to rejoice in the freedom from the diktats of fashion and the lustful male gaze the veil gives them, so perhaps the real issue is less the veil itself than the freedom to wear it—or not.

The attire is certainly impractical. Full veils make it difficult to see and the *abaya* restricts mobility. In the somewhat erratically paved Saudi streets, women tripping over their robes are a frequent sight, and not a few are run over at night because the black makes them hard to spot. By day, black is the most heat-absorbent color, and at 104°F (40°C) that is no laughing matter.

For the time being, women working in hospitals and other quasi-official institutions wear a veil that covers the face. Generally, in the Wahhabi heartland including Riyadh, women are rarely seen out, and if so are fully veiled. In Jeddah, fashionable women adopt a variety of styles, from a loose veil covering most of the hair to a stylishly piled scarf that covers the lower half of the face. There, a full veil leaving just slits for the eyes usually marks a woman as a visitor from elsewhere.

Western women should wear an *abaya* and a token head covering to avoid the attentions of officialdom. Filipinas, many of whom work as nurses in the kingdom, tend to be aggressive in their defiance of the veil, at work or out on the town, but they are probably a law unto themselves.

Guardianship

In tribal custom, it is widely considered to bring shame on a man if his wife's or sister's name is uttered in public. To alert girls when school is out that the guardian who has come to pick them up has arrived at the gates, for example, he will call out his own name over the public-address system. Women who have given birth are commonly referred to as Umm (mother of) followed by the name of their first-born, say Umm Mohammed, rather than their given name.

By law, a woman must be accompanied by a male guardian when she leaves the house. In conservative families, this can mean that women are essentially prisoners in the home; groups of young women from more liberal families can be seen out shopping, with one of them holding the hand of a small boy—their *mahram* for the day. Again, in Jeddah this requirement is widely ignored in upscale malls and downtown markets, certainly by foreign women, but in the rest of the kingdom it is often strictly enforced. On the whole, women's social life is frequently limited to visiting other female friends and relatives in the women's quarters of another family home.

Saudi women have found an unlikely champion in the form of the archconservative interior minister Prince Naif. In 2001, relying on his good standing with the *ulema*, he pushed through separate picture ID cards for women. Until then, women had been subentries without photos in their husband's or father's identity papers. In a court of law, they were expected to appear, silent, before a judge flanked by two male guardians who would testify to their identity. This inevitably gave rise to massive fraud, and women were habitually swindled out of their inheritance. All that was needed was for two interested parties to turn up with a veiled figure, claim she was so-and-so and award themselves power of attorney. The picture IDs put an end to that—except for the many women whose guardians refuse to sign their authorization for a picture ID.

In business, women also need the representation of a guardian. However, market forces have made things somewhat easier for them. By one widely publicized estimate, some US $30 billion lie idle in Saudi women's bank accounts—a fact that has given rise to a flurry of activity in the kingdom's influential chambers of commerce, which fill an important gap in the absence of democratic institutions, to encourage women to activate the money by investing it. In the big cities, they have set up one-stop "windows" to facilitate the business dealings of their women members. No such convenience exists, needless to say, for women without capital.

Education and Work

Public education for girls, on a voluntary basis, was introduced over a great outcry from conservatives in 1960, by King Faisal and his wife Queen Effat— an elite private girls' institute in Jeddah that is probably the closest the kingdom has to a Western-style liberal arts college is named after her. Until recently, girls' education came under a separate religious directorate, but this proved disastrous, and it has now been handed over to the Education Ministry. At university level, not all subjects are available in the women's sections.

Younger Saudi women, like women elsewhere, embraced their new educational opportunities with a vengeance and tend to be vastly better educated than their male counterparts. But they have few opportunities to put their skills to use.

Jobs open to women are largely confined to the health service and teaching. There is famously a Saudi woman who flies planes but may not drive a car: Hanadi Hindi is a pilot for a company belonging to one of the world's richest men, the liberal-minded Prince Alwaleed ibn Talal. But others work mostly as hospital receptionists or nurses or teach in girls' schools. There are also women academics teaching other women, and an increasing number of journalists and columnists. Most of them were educated abroad.

The problem is that women who want to work need the consent of their male guardian. When that guardian is a reasonable man, as many are, it's a minor administrative inconvenience. But if not, they have no other recourse.

Escape and Change

Women who can afford it get around the prohibition on driving by employing a driver, invariably a foreigner. Paradoxically, that is usually the only unrelated male they can be safely alone with. When lone women of any age, fully veiled though they may be, are driven around town by their driver, they are often subject to harassment from frustrated young men in their cars, who will swerve across several lanes to cruise alongside them, craning for a look and shouting obscenities.

In a famous incident in 1990, a group of educated women went for a protest drive in their cars in Riyadh. A barrage of condemnation from the *ulema* followed—placated again by Prince Naif with the remark that the women had been merely "stupid": most of them lost their jobs.

That leaves foreign countries. Saudi men escaping over the causeway to comparatively liberal Bahrain have been known to let their wife take the wheel halfway across the water. In much the same way, deeply veiled figures can be seen making a beeline for the rest room as soon as their plane leaves Saudi airspace, only to emerge minutes later from their chrysalis in revealing Western fashions. Against that, however, is the familiar image of fully veiled Saudi women picking their way through the baking streets or chilled malls of popular tourist destinations from LA to Singapore, three steps behind their guardian.

Since physical education is banned in girls' schools and eating is one of the few pastimes in which they are free to indulge, many Saudi women suffer from health problems, often related to obesity. From London to Bangkok, private hospitals are cashing in on a Saudi health tourism boom— rumor has it that not all Saudi women who seek treatment abroad are ill in any true medical sense.

In public debate, feminists across the Muslim world have largely abandoned Western arguments of liberation. Instead, they seek an ally in the religion they are often told will not permit them any rights. Not so, they say, citing the crucial role women played in the time of the Prophet. Mohammed's favorite wife, Aisha, is said to have led soldiers into battle, they point out, and is a key source of *hadith*, the traditions of the Prophet's words and deeds that form the broader canonical basis of Islam. The debate, as they say, continues.

ATTITUDES TOWARD FOREIGNERS

For the Arabs, hospitality is a matter of honor and a sacred duty. The main reason for this is that the Bedouin lived in a desert environment where nomads depended on each other's hospitality to survive thirst, hunger, and sudden raids or enemy attacks. But Islam extends this to anyone living in Muslim lands under a "covenant" that guarantees them the protection of their hosts. In theory at least, Saudis will have a sense that they are charged with your welfare and safety.

But prejudices die hard, and in a culture that stresses tradition as theirs does, other ingrained beliefs and practices are difficult to overcome. Bear in mind that slavery was not abolished until the 1960s. One of the areas where the kingdom's inherent contradictions are most startlingly at work is in the attitude to foreigners.

The orthodoxy is that foreign influence is something to be shunned lest it pollute the kingdom's Islamic and Arab "purity." In a country one-fifth of whose population are foreigners, this is no easy task, and the guardians of purity have a constant battle on their hands, helped no doubt by the Saudi tendency to wall themselves in. Yet the reality is that Saudis would now be wholly lost without their American cars, their Lebanese food, and the Indians and Filipinos who attend to their daily needs.

Westerners

Visitors and expatriates from the West can look forward to a respectful treatment they rarely encounter at home. Their path through the kingdom's Byzantine bureaucracy will be smoothed at every turn in a way few Saudis themselves can dream of, and their material comforts are virtually guaranteed. Saudis have a particularly high opinion of Americans. Theirs is essentially a bipolar world—a mental Saudi map of the world would show two equal bulging areas, the USA and the Middle East, surrounded by great empty oceans.

It is American products Saudis trust most. Most of their enormous arms acquisitions come of course from the USA, and nowhere outside the USA do so many ungainly, gas-guzzling American cars fill the streets. The supermarket shelves groan with American foods, and only recently have Korean electronics started replacing their equivalents from Whirlpool and General Electric.

Young Saudis, like young people anywhere, watch MTV, listen to American pop music, and dress in fashions they associate with the Land of the Free. Before 9/11, many looked forward to escaping to the USA from the boredom at home. When they grow older, they may take the wife to Hardee's for a treat or pick up massive family meals at McDonalds.

None of that affects an equally widely held belief that America is the Great Satan, the source, along with Israel, of all the troubles of the Arab world, and a sink of unimaginable—and thus wickedly alluring—corruption. Even the Coke-sipping, Levis-wearing youngsters in the cities talk knowledgeably of the perniciousness of US foreign policy and are as likely as their religious leaders to believe that America is involved in a plot to disenfranchise them—"franchise" being perhaps the operative word.

Yet while Saudis may discuss politics with you, they will be careful to make you understand that they hold no grudge against you personally. Whether your homeland is a staunch ally in America's "war on terror" or not, you can expect to be treated with courtesy, or at worst indifference. There will be some curious glances but at no point, it should be stressed, any hostility as you go about your daily life—unless you march straight into an Islamist slum in Buraidah, in the interior. Indeed, some Saudi and US commentators hold the improbable view that the people of the two countries have more in common with each other than with many other nations; family values are often cited.

There are an estimated 27,000 Americans in Saudi Arabia, mostly working for the oil giant Saudi Aramco and various defense contractors like Vinnell, who earn the highest salaries of any foreigners in the kingdom. Next come some 25,000 Britons—doctors, engineers working for British Aerospace, and the like—followed by several thousand other EU citizens dispatched by companies from their home countries. Almost invariably, they are accommodated in walled compounds, now heavily guarded, where the kingdom's restrictions do not apply.

While some wealthy young Saudis and some members of the elite are happy to chat to Westerners, especially when they have been educated abroad, ordinary Saudis (*pace* one reader commenting on a recent book about the kingdom) "do not talk to foreigners." And it is true that Saudis are much less outgoing than other Arabs, mostly out of shyness and a respect for the privacy they also accord each other: interaction outside a professional context is limited. Westerners, in other words, can expect to be left alone by their hosts if they so choose.

Easterners

Laborers from Asian countries sweep the tarmac of Saudi streets dressed in orange jumpsuits in the 104°F (40°C) heat all day. At night, many are herded into concrete cells with a minuscule window with five other workers, where they may bunk down on a bare mattress. Often the pay (if they get paid at all) is barely enough to take care of their most basic needs, let alone send any money home to their family thousands of miles away, who have got into debt to send them here. Many need to find other, illegal menial work to make ends meet, but when they do, they live in fear of arrest and a beating.

Asian women may be virtual prisoners in their employer's home, working sixteen hours a day for demanding employers, who sometimes slap them around. The men may expect to have their way with them, or even rape them if they refuse. Laborers often don't see their family or home country for many years. Some try to run away, of course, but their employers confiscate their identity papers, and their country's embassy has its hands full with hundreds of others like them and is unlikely to be of much help.

These are unfortunately not rare cases. The embassies of Indonesia and Sri Lanka have set up special accommodation for so-called "runaway maids," and the newspapers—never usually anxious to report anything that might reflect negatively on the kingdom—are full of stories about Indians, Pakistanis, and Bangladeshis owed months of their minuscule pay and held in degrading conditions. Why deny it? The Saudi attitude to, and treatment of, the millions of South and Southeast Asians and even workers from poorer Arab countries like Egypt is nothing to be proud of.

Of course, many are treated perfectly adequately by their employers. But Saudis of all classes show little respect toward waiters from the Philippines—aping their accents, snapping their fingers at them—and bark at Pakistani drivers, Bangladeshi cleaners, and highly qualified Indian professionals in a way that would get them into serious trouble anywhere else.

This is ironic, since the kingdom could do without most of the Westerners there but would literally come to a standstill without the Asians who do all the essential work: transporting, selling, and cooking their food, caring for their health, manning their gas stations, maintaining their infrastructure—and even staffing a navy where all officers are Saudi but all able seamen Filipino. Repeated attempts to "Saudize" the labor market have fallen flat because Saudis simply cannot be persuaded to do the work.

More enlightened Saudi employers tend to pity Asian guest workers for coming from the "Third World" and see them as childlike (this is echoed in the Saudi government's zeal for spreading Wahhabi Islam to corners of the Earth with more evolved traditions). But few, no matter how superficially sophisticated or Westernized, treat them as equals.

The main reasons probably lie in poor education, the recent memory of slavery, the hierarchical structure of Saudi society itself, and the special status Saudis believe their nation enjoys in the Muslim world (most of the guest workers, after all, come from Muslim countries). Of course, another element feeds into it as well: Saudis are in a way painfully aware of the low esteem in which Arabs are held in the West, and as ever the underdog develops a tendency to take it out on those even lower down in the pecking order.

Visitors from the West should be very careful not to fall into the same behavior. Raising the matter with your hosts would in many ways be unhelpful, but it costs nothing to say "please" and "thank you" when you are being served—and tips are also welcome.

RESTRICTIONS ON NON-MUSLIMS

Non-Muslims are forbidden from entering the holy cities of Mecca and Medina, and in these days of constant patrols and Muslim anger at the West, it is not a good idea to try. Resident expatriates are easily identified by religion on their work permit, or *iqama*: green for Muslims, red for infidels. The boundary is a 30-mile (48-km) radius around the holy cities, and road signs on the approach from Jeddah make it abundantly clear where to turn off.

Saudi Arabia is also one of a handful of Muslim countries that ban non-Muslims from their mosques, so any sightseeing will have to be limited to the exterior. And while the Saudi government is an enthusiastic sponsor of mosques in infidel lands, it blocks all traffic in the other direction. There are, to be sure, clandestine churches, but outside Western compounds those who run or frequent them are liable to arrest and worse.

The Authorized Version in your carry-on luggage is probably safe if your skin is white, but it is best not to try and import Bibles in quantity, no matter what the ostensible purpose (the same, of course, goes for the sacred texts of other religions). Buddhist or, say, Wiccan texts are safe simply because the customs officer would have no idea what they are, but make sure they come with a neutral cover.

In matters of religion generally, bear in mind that the punishment for apostasy is death, so any perceived attempt to persuade Muslims to abandon their faith for another will be dealt with severely.

In the unlikely event that romance should blossom in the desert, it is non-Muslim men who find themselves at a greater disadvantage. By the

JEWS

Many Saudis are anti-Semitic, making no distinction between the state of Israel and Jews living there or elsewhere. Like many other Arabs, they believe there is a Zionist conspiracy afoot to establish a Greater Israel "from the Euphrates to the Nile" with the help of America. According to one human rights watchdog, Saudi textbooks still teach the "Protocols of the Elders of Zion" (a hoary anti-Semitic forgery of the tsarist secret police) as a genuine Jewish plot to dominate the world. Some educational and religious texts, hard-line sermons, and newspaper columns routinely denounce and call for the killing of Jews—although, Arabic being a flowery language, this should be understood as an expression of anger at Israel rather than an actual call to arms. When translating from Arabic, translators tend to render *al-yahood* (Jews) as "Zionists," but that is disingenuous.

Saudi reading of Shariah law, it is extremely difficult if not impossible for a Saudi woman to marry a foreigner, even if the man is a Muslim or converts to Islam. Usually the woman would have to relinquish her Saudi citizenship and resign herself to exile. Marrying an unrepentant non-Muslim would automatically make her an apostate.

Any non-Muslim woman who marries a Saudi is assumed to have converted to Islam, but bear in mind that this automatically makes her subject to the full force of Saudi law—any children are under the sole authority of the father, for example. Western embassies tend to take a dim view of *Not Without My Daughter*-style second thoughts.

EDUCATION AND WORK

The literacy rate in Saudi Arabia has been estimated—by the CIA—at 84.7 percent for males and 70.8 percent for females. In the kingdom's early years, education was offered in a handful of *madrasas*, or Islamic schools, and the rest was up to individual parents. Now, public elementary and secondary education is universal and free. But it is not compulsory, and a decade ago the estimate was that some 61 percent of children attended. Population growth, and the attendant competition for available jobs, means that this figure has now risen substantially. Of course, students are strictly segregated.

Education remains heavily centered around Islam. Elementary schoolchildren, for instance, study Islam—and that mostly means memorizing the Koran—for nine periods a week, and have only twelve for everything else, from languages to math. All curricula must conform to Shariah law and the

Koran, and an ingrained fear of knowledge among the *ulema* still outweighs the benefits other branches of government may see in it.

Use of the cane has been abolished, but teachers remain figures of unquestioned authority to ordinary people, except when they go so far overboard in disciplining students that they attract media attention—in one widely publicized case, making children stand for hours in the burning sun for some infraction. Yet the children of the wealthy sometimes expect to bribe, threaten, and wheedle adequate marks from their teachers, and many have their homework done by servants. Independent thought is not encouraged, both as a result of Wahhabi orthodoxy and because it would overtax many of the kingdom's teachers.

Most of the kingdom's nine universities turn out a vast and unemployable number of religious scholars but not nearly enough computer programmers, engineers, and accountants; the notable exception is the oil-industry-oriented King Fahd University of Petroleum and Minerals in Dhahran. Government efforts to rectify this are often thwarted by the *ulema* and a lack of qualified academic staff. This is one reason that more and more commercial colleges are springing up, but these tend to be hampered by the students' conviction that they are buying an education and are therefore entitled to top marks for no effort.

Needless to say, for bright, motivated students the system offers a perfectly adequate framework. The problem is with the others. Traditionally, parents who can afford it have their children educated abroad. Until recently, that often meant lesser, profit-making schools and universities in the USA, with mixed results. Post-9/11, the trend is to send more students to Malaysia and other parts of Muslim Asia. Some also go to schools and universities in parts of the Middle East with a tradition of educational excellence, such as Lebanon, or, for the seriously rich and the royals, Britain's public schools and the *Internate* of Switzerland.

Change is coming, slowly, through economic demands—chambers of commerce calling for graduates their member firms don't have to train from scratch, for example—but a recent setback has been the appointment of a religious hard-liner as education minister. Overall, the poor state of education is one reason observers have called the kingdom's burgeoning young population a "tinderbox."

When they graduate, as growing numbers do, most young Saudi men expect to find a job in management or the civil service. The years of plenty after the oil boom have ingrained in them a notion that they will be *mudir*—the boss—and they are accordingly reluctant to put in hard work for less. While there are hardworking Saudis, especially from less privileged backgrounds, the work ethic is on the whole anything but Calvinist. The result is that many employers prefer to hire guest workers, and orders from above to hire more Saudis are habitually ignored.

chapter three

CUSTOMS & TRADITIONS

CALENDARS

The Saudi year is measured by the Muslim lunar calendar from the birth of Islam, though the kingdom's National Day is marked in the Gregorian calendar. Thus 2008 is 1428/29 *Hijra* (after Mohammed's emigration from Mecca to Medina), the lunar year having about 354 days— there is a prohibition on intercalary or leap months in the Koran. Newspapers list both *Hijra* and CE, while banks and other big businesses tend to use the Gregorian calendar for convenience.

Friday is the day of rest, with Thursday a half day in banks and government offices.

RAMADAN

The month of Ramadan, the ninth month of the Islamic calendar during which the Koran was revealed, is dedicated to the duty of fasting, to prayers, and to charity. All able-bodied adults must fast from sunrise to sunset during the whole month, though menstruating women are excused if they make up the lost days later. Sex is also forbidden from dawn to dusk.

The month begins with the sighting of the new moon, which must literally be *sighted* by several reliable witnesses, rather than calculated by astronomical means, for Ramadan to start and end. This can give rise to disputes, and dates may vary in different countries, as in 2007, when Saudis fasted for a day longer than most other Muslims, who took their cue from authorities elsewhere.

At sunset, the fast is broken with the *iftar* meal, which traditionally consists of a handful of dates and a drink of water or apricot juice. The wealthy set up long *iftar* tables on their property, and in theory everyone is welcome to eat. Driving at *iftar* time is hazardous, with everyone impatient (not to say frenzied) to pick up a dish of lentil or bean soup—*fuul*—and get

home. In the small hours, people gather again for the lavish *suhour* meal.

In practice, the feast continues throughout the night. It is now more common for people to put on weight during the fasting month than to lose it, nibbling on special Ramadan treats such as date cakes, or *kalaj*, a pastry of thin sheets of dough dipped in milk, stuffed with a heavy cream, deep-fried, and sprinkled with sugar or drizzled with honey. Recently, a number of enterprising women in Jeddah have taken to selling home-cooked food in specially erected tents.

Those who can afford it simply sleep through the daylight hours. Night turns into day: the streets and mosques are lit up with festive decorations—the writing with light, or *mahya*—and uncharacteristically teeming with people. Shops, malls, and restaurants stay open until dawn and do a roaring trade.

For the pious, the nights of the last week of Ramadan are spent in prayer, especially the Night of Light (*Leilat al-Qadr*), when beautifully sung recitations of the entire Koran ring nonstop from certain mosques. Daylight activities tend to be sluggish, particularly toward the end of the month, when those who do work are exhausted after weeks of letting no food or even water pass their lips from dawn till dusk. Non-Muslims should be careful not to be seen eating in public while others fast.

Besides eating, Saudis also spend the month watching massively popular Ramadan soaps from across the region, which sometimes broach audacious subjects such as adultery. Especially loved, despite condemnations from above, is a homegrown sitcom called *Tash ma Tash* that mocks, among other things, Islamists as bumbling idiots and plays off the regional and tribal idiosyncrasies of its cast.

At the sighting of the new moon, Ramadan culminates in the holiday of Eid al-Fitr.

THE HAJJ

During the lunar month of Dhul-Hijjah, some two million Muslims make their way to the kingdom and perform the rituals of pilgrimage dressed, as the Koran instructs, in two white, seamless garments. As we have seen, the origins of the pilgrimage go back to pre-Islamic times, but it was fully assimilated as the central event of the Islamic year. The Koran tells every able-bodied Muslim to perform the Hajj at least once in a lifetime, and for many it is a lifelong ambition.

Pilgrims follow in the footsteps of the Prophet Mohammed: the sacred sites along the pilgrimage route formed the backdrop to the most important events of his life.

Pilgrims spend a night in prayer near the town of Mina, which turns into an enormous tent city. On the morning of the following day, they proceed to the Plain of Arafat, where they perform the central ritual of the Hajj, the standing prayer, from noon to sunset.

Back in Mecca, the rituals include the *tawaf*, which consists of walking counterclockwise seven times around the Kaaba. This is a cuboid structure at the center of the Grand Mosque roughly facing the four points of the compass, which contains a black stone believed to be a meteorite fragment, and is covered with a black silk cloth. According to the Koran, the structure was built by Ibrahim (Abraham) and his son Ishmael (Isaac); and the Prophet, when he established Islam, cleared it of the pagan idols the Meccans had housed there. All Muslims, wherever they are in the world, face the Kaaba when they pray.

Another ritual in the Grand Mosque compound is the *sa'i*, walking seven times back and forth between the hills of Safa and Marwah— a reenactment of the search of Hagar, Ibrahim's wife, for water for Ishmael before the Zamzam well there was revealed to her. Many pilgrims also drink from the well.

Managing the Pilgrimage
Marshaling these huge numbers of pilgrims is the kingdom's great logistical achievement. While accidents do occur—a particularly dangerous spot for stampedes is Jamrat, a pillar representing the devil and ritually stoned by pilgrims—Saudis say it is a miracle that they do not happen more frequently. Still, in 2006 some 600 pilgrims died while performing the Hajj, 362 of them at Jamrat.

There is a government minister solely responsible for Hajj affairs, who allots annual quotas to Muslim countries for the number of pilgrims they may send. Airport buildings, roads, water, and health facilities are provided for pilgrims, notably the tented Hajj terminal at King Abdul Aziz Airport in Jeddah. The government also distributes bottled water, juice, and boxed lunches during the climbing of Mount Arafat and stations ambulances in strategic locations.

It also relieves pilgrims of the task of having to slaughter a sacrificial beast. The Islamic Development Bank now sells coupons for animals, which are chosen by the pilgrim and then slaughtered, processed, and frozen for distribution among the poor, first in Mecca and then throughout the rest of the Muslim world.

The Hajj is an important source of income for the Hijaz. Many pilgrims will also do some shopping for electronics and textiles in Jeddah, for centuries the port of entry and traditionally reliant on the Hajj and Umrah (or lesser pilgrimage) for its economy. In the old days, the local emir used to exact exorbitant taxes on pilgrims in return for his "protection." Jeddah's textile traders say they essentially do a year's business during the month and complain about government efforts to marshal pilgrims solely along the sacred routes.

The city of Mecca has, as one writer puts it, developed into a kind of "Las Vegas of Islam" with a skyline to match, its massive condominium and hotel developments dwarfing the minarets of the Grand Mosque. Some wealthy Saudis regard the pilgrimage as a status symbol, performing it more frequently than the Koran instructs—some go every year.

NATIONAL HOLIDAYS
Eid al-Fitr

This three-day festival signifying the breaking of the fast falls on the new moon at the end of Ramadan; the date depends on the sighting of the new moon with the naked eye around sunset. False alarms are common, what with cloud cover and other vagaries— followed by groans when people realize the mistake.

When Eid al-Fitr comes, everyone puts on their best clothes. Before a short communal prayer in the early morning every Muslim must pay *zakat*, or alms, donating food for the poor or a cash equivalent that is collected at mosques. Wealthy Saudis give lavishly to charity, and their donations have sometimes gone to dubious organizations. The prayer is followed by a sermon. The faithful exchange hugs to a cry of "*Eid mubarak*," and then feast and visit relatives and friends.

As in the rest of the world, for many Saudis text messages have replaced visits in the flesh. And as elsewhere, many Saudis use the holiday—one of only three they can officially observe—to go on vacation abroad. In the week or so following Ramadan, shops tend to be shuttered and the streets are even more deserted than usual.

Eid al-Adha

Again a three-day holiday, this marks the end of the official Hajj, when pilgrims descend from Mount Arafat. Men, women, and children again dress in their best clothes and perform the Eid prayer. Muslims who can afford it slaughter their best domestic animals—usually sheep but also camels, cows, and goats—or more likely buy an animal for the purpose. Since the animal is traditionally bled out, this can be a rather gory affair for some Western sensibilities.

The event celebrates Ibrahim's willingness to sacrifice his son Ishmael at Marwah (Abraham and Isaac at Mount Moriah in the Judaeo-Christian tradition). According to the Koran, two-thirds of the meat from the sacrificial animal is given to the poor and hungry so all members of the Muslim *ummah* can join the feast. The remainder is cooked for a big family celebration. Coming roughly seventy days after Eid al-Fitr, the holiday these days falls at the end of the Gregorian year, around December 8 in 2008 and November 27 in 2009.

Saudi National Day

This falls on the rare Gregorian date of September 23 to mark the kingdom's foundation in 1932.

There has been long debate with religious hard-liners as to whether it should be permitted at all: Islam, as they never tire of pointing put, has only two holidays, Eid al-Fitr and Eid al-Adha. Still, it has recently become a day off work and is made up on Saturday if it falls on a Friday.

Ordinary Saudis welcome the day off but don't otherwise observe it, though schoolchildren may attend ceremonies and officials make speeches.

Season's Greetings

Many young Saudis borrow Western occasions like Valentine's Day, Christmas, and birthdays to give each other presents, perhaps in a bid to feel more part of the wider world. Cue condemnation and dire warnings from the *ulema*. In the run-up to February 14, 2004, the *mutawwa* were tasked with confiscating any teddy bears, plastic roses, and other gifts containing the color red if they spotted them in the shops.

SUPERSTITION

Despite the exhortations of some religious leaders, many Saudis are deeply superstitious. They live in particular fear of the evil eye—especially envy—and talismans to ward it off adorn cars and shop windows. These are either in the shape of a single eye, often painted on the back of trucks, or little

Koranic scrolls that dangle from the rear mirror or sit in display windows. The word *Mashallah* (praise be to God) is believed to fend off the evil eye and is therefore used to congratulate someone on good luck or an achievement.

Saudis are also afraid of witchcraft, which is occasionally punished by the courts—in fact, probably code for a crackdown on Shiites or Christians. However, it is not unknown for people to seek out black magic in the slums to help them in an endeavor.

Before embarking on a task, from starting their car to sitting down to a meal, people invoke divine protection by muttering the first word of the Koran, "*Bismillah*"—in the name of God. This is also said if they drop something, for fear that the devil may have snatched at it from below. Perhaps it is because of such quasi-Islamic defenses that superstition survives the austerity of Wahhabi belief.

A special case is the belief in *djinn*, or demons. Since they are mentioned in the Koran—indeed, Islam is revealed to "men and djinn"—it does not rate as a superstition at all, especially in the literalism of Wahhabi Islam. Worldly Saudis tend to avoid discussing the matter.

Belief in *kismet* (fate) is very strong, to the point where Arabs are often accused of fatalism: everything is ordained and will happen *inshallah*, if God wills. But against that stands the popular proverb, "Trust the Lord, but tether your camel!"

MAKING FRIENDS

chapter four

FRIENDSHIP

After family and tribe, friendship is the most important tie that binds Saudis. The major friendships are formed early, at school, and can last a lifetime. In a segregated environment, they are often intense and exclusive and can have a romantic flavor—close friends are described as couples by their peers—that gradually wears off as the protagonists get married and have children of their own.

Among males, they also often take the form of a mentor–protégé relationship across generations, and again they outlive any romantic overtones when the younger partner grows a beard and starts a family. The friendships Saudis form later in life are often in the nature of patron–client relationships.

After the initial reticence that sets them apart from other Arabs—a mixture of shyness and respect for privacy—many Saudis are open to establishing friendships with Westerners. These will take time to build: the proverb Saudis like to cite in almost every context is "patience is a virtue." The best idea is simply to wait with an open mind and let them come to you: being too eager might frighten Saudis off; at the same time, they may interpret reticence on your part as meaning that you want to be left alone.

Once a friendship has been built, it is difficult to undo and can survive disappointments and betrayals that would swiftly end it in the West. It's one of the great puzzles of Saudi Arabia that a wrong you have done a friend (or had done to you) will simply be forgotten. After an appropriate interval for sulking, you can suddenly find yourself embraced as if nothing had happened.

Friends for Life

An example of the enduring value of Saudi friendships is the murdered Lebanese prime minister Rafiq Hariri, who arrived in the kingdom in 1965 with nothing but became rich beyond his wildest dreams in construction and publishing there thanks to patronage from the royal family. In 1978 Hariri became a Saudi citizen and the kingdom's emissary to Lebanon. Once back in Beirut and leading his country, he made frequent trips to Saudi Arabia and apparently never went home empty-handed.

Loyalty to friends is observed in deed more than in word. Saudis can comprehensively disparage one friend when talking to another or even to a casual acquaintance in terms that suggest they hardly know each other. Don't be taken in: an established friendship will almost always take precedence over a new acquaintanceship or mere business ties.

MEETING SAUDIS

For most visitors, the first and sometimes only point of contact with Saudis is professional, in the workplace, with business partners or, for the many foreign teachers, with students. In the cities, it is unusual to meet ordinary Saudis in any other way. As previously mentioned, Saudis are much less outgoing than other Arabs and value their privacy highly; they rarely strike up a conversation with a stranger in a café, for example, or if they do will be content with a brief exchange. A typical chat might go like this: [Long quizzical stare] "Where do you come from?" [Foreigner names country.] "Welcome." [The end.]

However, many Saudis have been educated abroad or have lived and done business in the West, and they may be happy to linger for a chat at work and in due course strike up an easy acquaintanceship or friendship. How far this develops depends partly on you, just as it would at home. Friendships among Saudis are often patron–client relationships—where the person with the higher status, greater age, or more money looks after the other in return for loyalty—so expatriates may also find themselves adopted by their boss if there is a mutual liking.

Across genders, meeting strangers is even rarer outside work. Western men should be sensitive as Saudi women can be very conservative. Western women will find Saudi men very respectful according to their understanding of Western standards. As it happens, a Western woman is probably safer here than in some other countries, where any blonde is considered fair game. Saudi men may practice their considerable charms, but they are unlikely to undress Western women with their eyes, less still attempt to grope them.

In parts of the country that see few Westerners, local dignitaries may still feel that they are charged with a guest's welfare and may welcome him as it were on behalf of the town, and even invite him to their home so he is safely looked after during his stay.

Saudis are painfully aware of their negative image in the West, and of the tendency of Western expatriates to retreat to the safety of their compounds. A sure way to their hearts is to take an interest in their culture, or simply to be willing to suspend judgement and engage with them.

GREETINGS

Polite greetings are important, but in contrast to other Asian countries, no elaborate show of courtesy is required. Saudis are oddly egalitarian in some ways, and it isn't uncommon for a wealthy customer in the supermarket to shake hands with the (Saudi) salesman over the cold-cuts counter. Indeed, Saudi men are great shakers of hands and will expect to shake hands, firmly, at every meeting and parting.

More traditional Saudis will then place their hand over their heart, and it would be polite for visitors to do the same. Westernized Saudis dispense with this part of the ritual and may think it rather peculiar if you insist on the pantomime: the safest bet is simply to copy what a new acquaintance does. Among themselves, Saudi men who know each other well kiss one another on the cheek, but they are perfectly conscious that this is their way and not everyone else's.

A Western man should not offer his hand to a Saudi woman he does not know well, but simply wait to see if she extends her hand. Never try to shake hands with a woman in the street.

The formal greeting is *salaam aleikum*, "peace be with you"—or, in the regal way some Saudis seem to adopt as a status symbol, a rolling *as-salaam-u aleikum*—to be answered with *wa aleikum salaam*, "and peace be with you." Now, strictly speaking, that is the greeting among

Muslims, and if a Westerner offers it, some not-so-friendly Saudis may refuse to return it, answering instead with a crisp "Hi." You would be justified in thinking this rude and may proceed accordingly.

Then there is the more informal *ahlan*, "hello"—short for *ahlan wa sahlan*, "my home and my family (are at your disposal)"—to be answered likewise, and *marhaba*, ditto.

HOSPITALITY AND INVITATIONS

In due course, visitors may find themselves invited to a restaurant or someone's home. Remember that Saudis are Asians, so any vague invitation—"You must visit"—or promise of an impending outing is not to be taken at face value. Saudis love to make such promises, the popular phrase being, "We will sit together." Don't be disappointed if they never materialize: the person making them probably just means to express general goodwill.

When the invitation is genuine, it will have a firm time and date attached. Refusal, of course, would be considered hurtful unless you have a good excuse and can suggest another time. If you suffer from extreme social phobia, your Saudi acquaintance will probably intuit this and respect your wish to be left alone; otherwise, you should accept the invitation with good grace.

In a restaurant, the host will pay. Saudis have nothing but contempt for the notion of going Dutch, even among long-term friends and equals. Visitors made uncomfortable by this should wait their turn to invite their Saudi host out.

On Arrival

Invitations to someone's home offer a chance to experience how important hospitality is to a Saudi. People's behavior can vary widely, so the best thing is to play it by ear rather than arrive with any preconceived notion of a ritual to be got through. Visitors should use common sense, and if they're baffled, ask. Bear in mind that Saudi hosts will make allowances for a foreigner's cultural proclivities and adjust the occasion to what they think his needs are. There is usually no need to bring a gift.

Most Saudi homes that foreigners are likely to visit will have Western-style furniture (often in a style that has been described as Syrian baroque). A few basic rules: it is customary to take off your shoes when entering the house unless your host is wearing his. If sitting on cushions, don't point the soles of your feet at others. Generally accept what you are offered. This may include alcohol from a surprisingly well-stocked bar—a status symbol for some Saudi hosts—and unless you are a teetotaler, you might as well accept even if your host won't drink with you.

On arrival, you are more likely to be offered a cup of *kahwa*, aromatic coffee from unroasted coffee beans and spices in a thimble of a cup. After one or two cups, the way to indicate "enough" is to shake it from side to side.

A male visitor may or may not meet the womenfolk (or, as a woman, the menfolk), who have their separate quarters. It all depends how conservative or trusting the host is. If invited as a couple, you may be separated on arrival, to eat with your own gender. Comply with good grace.

The Meal

Dinner, after a suitable period of sitting around, could be almost anything, but is most likely to be a lavish spread of roast and barbecued meats and the inevitable *kabsa*—spiced rice with meat similar to India's biryani. If you don't know how to eat something, copy your host. There will be too much of everything, so eat heartily but stop when you are full. Your host will press you a little, out of politeness, but there is no force-feeding.

In the past, Arabs ate with their hands, using only the right since the left was reserved for personal hygiene. But now many Saudis—and most of those likely to invite foreigners—use cutlery and sit at a dining table. Don't worry too much about infractions of etiquette: your host will probably be far too concerned with your welfare and his duties to take umbrage. Some writers warn against admiring anything in your host's home lest it be offered to you as a gift; but in Saudi Arabia you would have to admire something very hard indeed if you wanted it.

The meal will probably take some time, culminating in a great variety of sweets. Since Saudis are great storytellers, visitors can leave much of the entertainment to their host, who may regale them with a welter of amusing anecdotes, many to be taken with a pinch of salt. Again, don't fret: things will be much more relaxed than they would be in a highly socially regimented country like, say, Korea or Japan. Let your host take the lead in the conversation to be on the safe side; most Saudis prefer talking to listening.

Some cultural barriers do loom large, such as when a host is moved to discuss women "man to man" in crude terms. If this gets too much, use your social skills to steer the conversation round to another topic.

There is usually not much after-dinner conversation, so once all the dishes have been cleared away, it is time to think of going home.

LIFE ON THE COMPOUND

The great majority of Western expatriates live in compounds. These housing estates were set up by agreement between the USA and the kingdom, originally to keep Western influence in, but increasingly to keep Saudi reality out. A few Saudis also prefer the relative freedom from the kingdom's restrictions they offer: here, no *abaya* needs to be worn, the sexes can mingle freely, and the shops stay open at prayer time. Home-brewed alcohol tends to be freely available.

The compounds vary from the lavish to the downright shabby, from accommodating hundreds of families to a few dozen, but as on most housing estates, the neighbors are too close, the walls are too thin, and petty jealousies and

quarrels enliven the otherwise unvarying routine. Almost all have a swimming pool, convenience store, gym, and other facilities. Long-term expatriates seem to look on compounds as status symbols and covet an apartment or villa in the more popular ones.

Westerners who have come to work will most likely live in compounds or can expect to spend a great deal of their social life in them. Many organize Thursday night parties where, often for a small set contribution, those invited can take part in the revels, usually a barbecue and drinks, sometimes more raucous fun. Home-brewed wine and beer tend to be freely available, and unless someone sells them off-site in quantity, the authorities turn a blind eye.

Expatriates are generally easygoing and welcoming to new arrivals, who will soon find themselves invited to one of these bashes as they meet other Westerners around the pool or at work—probably the best defense against the stultifying boredom that can grip even the best-intentioned stranger here.

In 2003, however, compounds in Riyadh suffered devastating terrorist attacks, and since then they have been guarded like fortresses, with a tank or two parked permanently outside the front gate. That has made life there even more unreal, and many residents in such siegelike conditions believe the Saudi cities they live in to be vastly more dangerous than they really are. It doesn't help that embassies like to issue security circulars exhorting people to "keep a low profile," stay indoors at prayer time, and so on.

Despite the terrorist attacks, Saudi cities remain among the safest in the world. If you live in a compound, try to go out as much as possible, especially after evening prayer, when the souks see as much life as they ever do—this is admittedly not much compared to London or Tokyo, but it offers at least a glimpse of how Saudis spend their evenings.

ASIAN EXPATRIATES

If you are curious about other cultures, you should make an effort to meet expats from India. There are some 1.4 million of these extraordinary people in the kingdom, making them a significant—and indispensable—Saudi minority in their own right. Many are highly educated and probably speak English better, or at least with more zest, than you do. And many have been in the kingdom for decades, so they can offer an inexhaustible store of local knowledge and lore.

For fun evenings with unusual food and interminable karaoke sessions, make friends in the Filipino community (you will have to develop a tolerance for high camp).

chapter five

PRIVATE & FAMILY LIFE

The family is the most important social institution in Saudi Arabia. Besides the tribe, it is the chief source of identity and the focus of loyalty. Among families, Saudis form a kind of alliance, as between states, based on common interests and lifestyles and usually socialize within this circle.

The family business—which is what most of them, including the regime, essentially remain—is open to sons, uncles, and (male) cousins, and forms the welfare safety net for all members of the extended family. In companies big and small, many Saudis will feel honor-bound to try and find a place for members of their circle. In the West, this would be considered nepotism, but Saudis do not see it this way.

The oldest male is usually the head of the extended family, and age is respected. Families are often vast, with a small army of children—not least because the government encouraged people to have as many children as possible in the wake of the oil boom, but also because, as cynics have pointed out, there is little else to do.

The kingdom's roads teem with massive SUVs that can transport the whole family, the rear windows often blacked out to shield the womenfolk from prying eyes. In a traffic dispute, a man who has just cut across four lanes may gesticulate in the general direction of his car and shout, "My family!" as if that explained everything.

How the Other Half Live

A Saudi government spokesman, Mansour Al-Turki, was quoted as telling a correspondent for the *LA Times*, "Being a Saudi doesn't mean you see every facet of Saudi society. Saudi men don't understand how Saudi women think. They have no idea, actually. Even my own family, my own mother or sister, they won't talk to me honestly."

Saudis are unusually jealous of their family's privacy. The joke goes that on a building site the wall around the plot is the first thing to go up, and this is generally true. The windows of family homes, however distant from the neighbors, are invariably mirrored glass or blacked out. There are none of the big family balconies you find in the cities of Egypt or Lebanon.

As a result, Saudis generally shun their neighbors and sometimes harbor terrible suspicions about them, their only source of information the gossip of their maids. This can be something of a problem in the three big cities, where people increasingly live on top of each other.

LIVING CONDITIONS
Homes

Jeddah's old town still has some of the traditional, intricately latticed verandas that allowed women in purdah to look out on the street without being seen. But that tradition has not survived. Most of Saudi Arabia is brand spanking new, or only falling to pieces because it was quite recently jerry-built.

Living conditions vary far more widely than in the other Gulf states. They range from the giant palaces of the royals that stretch over acres of built-up ground to the sprawling villas and well-appointed mansion flats of the wealthy, to dim, shabby apartments in the cities, to ramshackle farm hovels and slum huts. Cheap marble is everywhere, good architecture mostly absent. Whatever goes up, goes up in spite of the surroundings, not in harmony with it—perhaps inevitably in such inhospitable terrain.

There is growing poverty in the kingdom as the population explodes, and that is reflected in overcrowded housing. One royal or another is forever opening a new housing development for low-income families, but it is difficult to keep up.

Wherever Saudis live in their vast desert, the water supply is prone to breakdown and raw sewage can bubble out of the manholes. Roads are the kingdom's great pride and are smooth and well-maintained, but the side streets are often cracked and run-down, even in upscale areas.

Inside, homes usually have separate living areas for men and women. How strictly Saudis are segregated when they shut their doors behind them varies from family to family. Anecdotal evidence suggests that many people don't bother once nobody is looking, while others are utterly punctilious; a look at the layout of some city apartments suggests it can be a logistical nightmare.

In most homes, there is a sitting room with an upholstered and cushioned bench running the length of three walls where the host and guests can lounge over tea, coffee, sweets, and a *shisha*. There is often a separate dining area, usually nowadays with a Western-style table and chairs.

DAILY LIFE

Daily life is dictated by climate and religious duties. Everything comes to a standstill for the five daily prayers, when shops and restaurants pull their shutters down at the first call. That, rather than the time by the clock, marks the passing of the day. A mighty lull falls between the noonday (*dhuhr*) and the sunset (*maghrib*) prayers—even banks shut between 2:00 and 4:00 p.m.—because for most of the year it is simply too hot to go out.

It's only after *maghrib* that the cities come to life and families venture out to shop and eat in the relative cool of the evening. Things liven up further after *isha*, the prayer ninety minutes after sunset. Most people eat their family dinner at home after *maghrib* or *isha* and then go for a stroll, or they go to a restaurant at those times. By 11:00 p.m., residential streets are deserted again.

As yet, these ancient rhythms sit somewhat oddly with the eight-hour working day of modern offices, but most expatriates figure out their window of opportunity for bank business, for example, soon enough. Daily prayer times are printed in the newspapers.

Daily Necessities

Food, mostly imported, is in plentiful supply in hypermarkets of American dimensions. From Quaker Oats to sun-dried tomatoes, they stock everything under the sun—except pork—at very reasonable prices. Better-off Saudis prefer to shop here. But varieties of fresh meat, vegetables, pickles, cheese, dates, pastries, and other traditional foodstuffs are cheaper and often tastier in the souks, and many people from ordinary homes make their daily rounds here.

The shopping is often done by the lady of the house, accompanied by a maid or two and, depending on the region, a token male guardian. In the supermarket, she will simply point at the goods while the maid stocks the cart or, in the souk, picks up the bags.

Small neighborhood shops, or *bakalas*, stock a few canned and bagged items, not always (to the alarm of the newspapers) the right side of the sell-by date. Other necessities are also easily available in any quality and provenance.

SOCIAL GATHERINGS

Saudis enjoy social gatherings within their close circle. That can mean just sitting around shooting the breeze over endless cups of tea and *shisha* or, for influential people, a more formal meeting, or *majlis*, where important issues of the day are discussed. If the people attending them have a political role, they are sometimes attended by secret police who sit around looking awkward and fooling no one.

These meetings, for both men and women, are perhaps the only way that Saudi society can be said to connect, with members bringing uncensored news and gossip from their rounds outside the walls of the family home.

More informal meetings of this kind take place increasingly in restaurants or cafés with comfortable lounging areas for groups out of earshot of one another. Such cafés often have giant TV screens that show sports events and music videos. The patrons' *shishas* are constantly topped up from glowing censers until they call for a stop.

Weddings

For outsiders the notion of segregated wedding parties may seem extremely odd, but how could it be any other way? Weddings are less and less frequently held at home (unless the house is huge) and increasingly celebrated in hotels and special wedding halls, as elsewhere in Asia.

For men, the party traditionally consists of a big dinner where whole sheep and baby camels are roasted on a spit. When that is over, the groom and immediate members of the family leave to join the women's party. This is reportedly a great deal more fun and continues throughout the night and beyond. Until the men arrive, there is raucous singing and dancing to the complex drum rhythms of traditional music and modern pop in a festively decorated hall, with almost every female of any age joining in.

The groom's arrival around midnight is greeted by a shrill ululation from the assembled women. The groom is led to the dais and his new wife by his male relatives, who immediately make themselves scarce. He then gets to enjoy more dancing from the bride's close relatives. Once the couple have been escorted to their new home, the women carry on celebrating for two more nights at parties hosted by the couple's grandmothers.

Needless to say, such festivities are forbiddingly expensive. Increasingly, Islamic charities host mass weddings with a minimum of fuss, no dowry, and a few bites to eat to enable young people from low-income groups to get married.

YOUNG PEOPLE

As we have seen, people under twenty-five now make up two-thirds of the Saudi population. Often poorly educated and raised in a culture of entitlement, sometimes radicalized, and universally bored, they are a massive headache for a government led by mostly elderly men. Their education is strictly segregated (see page 80).

Boys

Many young Saudis are faced with a lifetime of unemployment or downward mobility as government subsidies dwindle, with shrinking opportunities at home and, even more so, abroad. At the same time, they see the world around them opening up ever wider: almost all Saudi homes have satellite TV, and that means illegal access to some two hundred channels, including hardcore European porn and underground Islamist propaganda.

They also have Internet access, and the plentiful blocks the Saudi government imposes are easily subverted through proxy servers. Many regard the Western content they see there with a mixture of envy, fascination, and moral horror. And many vent their frustration on Islamist hate sites.

What they lack is any outlet for their energies. Wherever the *shabab*, or "youth," go, the establishment understandably tries to shoo them away: for being a nuisance to cars carrying women on the road, for harassing families at popular picnic spots. Fads spring up—Riyadh's inner city was for a time haunted by daredevil in-line skaters—only to be mercilessly squashed. All Friday night, young men crowd the cities' main thoroughfares in their cars, going nowhere because there is nowhere to go.

The children of the wealthy gather in slick upscale cafés, where they watch skimpily dressed Lebanese pop stars on the giant TV screens and down coffee after coffee, while ordinary young Saudis lounge on carpets and cushions in huge, more traditional establishments.

Many hang around the malls in the evening, outside if they can't get in—often the malls have a "families only" policy that essentially means guards try to keep groups of young men out—to ogle and shadow girls and women on their shopping trips until the *mutawwa* disperse them.

Only the desert provides some refuge. Here, young men who can afford it take their tweaked four-wheel drives to let rip in the dunes, performing hair-raising stunts as they bring the camel races of yore screaming and crashing into the industrial age.

The graffiti in some abandoned farmhouses are a trace of their impromptu parties, a kind of all-male desert rave around the boom box.

Girls

Paradoxically, their more placid conduct means that girls have a little more access to the kingdom's few diversions: in Jeddah, where the *mutawwa* are hobbled by the local rulers, Saudi girls can go out mall shopping and visiting cafés in pairs or groups—and even, in some upscale malls, quite alone—or wander along the Corniche. Or they can round up a tame male guardian to chaperone them and their friends. Otherwise, they may gather in each other's homes and while away the time chatting and smoking.

As elsewhere, girls tend to be more serious about their education and better at learning—half of Saudi Arabia's university graduates are now women—and many reportedly read whatever they can get their hands on. They are more likely than their male counterparts to be eclectic in their culture consumption: it's *Sex and the City* all right, but also Milan Kundera and Paulo Coelho.

Of course, much of their talk revolves around men: again, they have the advantage because they can actually see them. A recent novel circulating in samizdat in the kingdom, *Girls of Riyadh* by Rajaa Alsanea, suggests their minds, like those of young women everywhere, turn mostly on romance.

Still, they tend to be resigned to the fact they may be married off young to a man they've barely met, and it's touch and go whether they will be permitted to work or able to find a job.

Dating

Information technology has multiplied the avenues for meeting members of the opposite sex. Time was when young men would drive up below the one-way mirrored windows of the family sections of certain cafés, holding up big pieces of cardboard with their phone number on them in case some girl took a fancy to them. Now, a fleeting encounter in the mall allows them to send their numbers via their phone's Bluetooth port. Romance is conducted by text message and e-mail. How far it can be taken is impossible for a Westerner to tell.

chapter **six**

TIME OUT

LEISURE

Saudis enjoy their leisure, and even a busy
workday is punctuated with periods of sitting
around, drinking tea, and cultivating relations
with colleagues. Weekends and evenings are
devoted to the family, be it a picnic, an outing to
the families-only amusement parks, or a feast at
home. Official unemployment is high, leading to a
great deal of enforced idleness, while many who
can afford it also lead lives of semi-leisure. Many
Saudis, in other words, cultivate the art of doing
nothing in particular.

But while often betraying no great curiosity about the outside world, they are also inveterate travelers for pleasure. America has been the traditional playground of the wealthy; now, after 9/11, Saudis throng popular tourist destinations in Egypt, Lebanon, and Asia.

Because Saudi Arabia is a place of family values and religion, for foreigners working in the kingdom it is a case of turning base carbon into gold. Finding something to occupy your spare time can take time and effort. An Internet connection is crucial; satellite TV is of the essence.

There are three official national holidays: Eid al-Fitr, Eid al-Adha, and Saudi National Day (see pages 90–2).

SOCIAL SPACE

The greatest culture shock in Saudi Arabia is the absence of social space. Built for cars, the newer areas—and almost all areas are new—have a forlorn aspect even at peak shopping times. Those used to other parts of the Middle East will be stunned by the absence of people in the streets.

Visitors who enjoy a stroll to soak up the life of a city should seek out the downtown souks and shopping centers where Arabs from elsewhere congregate. In Jeddah, this means the Souk al-Alawi and adjacent malls in the old town; in Riyadh, the Souk al-Thumairi near the Masmak fortress.

On the whole, the more downscale (and therefore frequented by Eastern expatriates) an area is, the more lively it is likely to be; and the more upscale and Saudi-dominated, the quieter.

Western men out on the town with their family, alas, can expect to be confined to the curtained, walled, and otherwise partitioned-off "family sections" of restaurants and cafés, severely limiting the opportunities for people-watching. In many cases, expatriate men are best off copying their Saudi hosts and sticking to their own gender. Western women's leisure activities are strictly circumscribed outside the home or compound.

SHOPPING FOR PLEASURE
Souks
The traditional markets or souks are good for handicrafts from other parts of the greater

Middle East—Saudis themselves were traditionally herders, traders, and raiders rather than sedentary craftsmen. What the host country does offer is a bewildering variety of dates in all stages from fresh to dried, dipped in chocolate, stuffed with almonds, covered in sesame seeds, and rolled in coconut. These are well worth giving a try.

Bedouin crafts include silver and amber ornaments; the inevitable pewter coffee pots can be picked up here too.

Saudis are lovers of scent. Both men and women use ample musk-based perfume, a rich Arabian tradition. Homes are scented with traditional *bukhour*, or incense, such as sandalwood (*oud*) chips or oil, heated on coals in distinctive four-sided, "turreted" censers. Whole sections of the downtown souks specialize in fragrances and paraphernalia: just follow the scent.

Rugs are also a good buy, from Persian to Afghan. Cheaper varieties are available in dedicated souks, while fine Persian silk carpets from Qom and Isfahan can be found in carpet shops. Expect to spend some time negotiating a reasonable price. Yet in contrast to other parts of the Middle East, there is otherwise not much haggling in the souk. Some vendors may offer a small discount of perhaps 5 to 10 percent if asked, but prices are essentially fixed.

DATES

Saudi Arabia exports little but oil, gas, . . . and dates. For millennia, these hardy and nutritious fruit were an essential part of the Bedouin diet because they  practically never go bad. A handful of dates goes a long way during a desert crossing. In dried form, they have a surprisingly complex taste reminiscent of marzipan.

The oasis of al-Hasa in the Eastern Province is the world's largest date-growing area. Connoisseurs consider the Khalasah, or Khlas, from al-Hasa the best dates in the world. But there is a multitude of regional varieties, which ripen in succession and vary in color from light brown to black. "The first crop is for the emir," the saying goes, "the last for the donkey."

Where other countries donate blankets to the needy, Saudi Arabia donates dates. In 2002, donations totaled nearly 881,849 short (US) tons (800,000 metric tons).

Malls

Under the *abaya*, Saudi women wear the world's great labels in all their revealing glory, and the Middle East's brightest colors. Fendi, Versace, Prada—all are available in the upscale malls, while regional gowns for older women in lemon yellow, lime green, and flamingo pink can be had further down the scale. For men, there are Boss and Diesel and the like, as well as lesser-known clothing brands from the subcontinent that can look profoundly camp to jaded Western eyes. Top brands often do a special line in *abayas* and *thobes* for their Gulf customers. As luxury brands go, they are quite reasonably priced, and a stroll around the gleaming high-end malls makes a refreshing break from the desert heat.

Electronics, especially from Korea and Japan, are also a good buy, the prices sometimes a little better than in more famous destinations such as Singapore and Bangkok. Home entertainment, of course, plays a crucial role in the kingdom. CD stores, for the iPod-less, can be remarkably well-stocked for a developing country, but import prices are steep. Thanks to the Filipino community, there is a glorious variety of old tape cassettes (presumably bought up as dead stock) of such karaoke favorites as Engelbert Humperdinck, the Carpenters, Frank Sinatra, and Kenny Rogers.

THE MUTAWWA

The religious police, or *mutawwa*, are officially known as the Committee for the Promotion of Virtue and Prevention of Vice, but their role is almost exclusively limited to the latter. Members are drawn from the lower-income groups; they thus combine zealotry with a minimal education and hatred of the rich, making them a highly effective tool to enforce the diktats of the *ulema* among the liberal tendency.

The *mutawwa* are instantly recognizable by the short *thobes* that identify them as fundamentalists under a traditional camel-hair coat, and by their vast unkempt beards. Invariably portly, they must be accompanied by ordinary police and usually trail a whippet-thin officer in khaki as they lumber through restaurants and malls to crack down on infractions.

In Jeddah, they have been more or less neutralized, but elsewhere they remain a powerful nuisance, turning off TVs, shouting at diners, and harassing women for not covering up sufficiently. Asian expatriates are particularly easy prey for these men.

They are also in charge of the kingdom's censorship, defacing foreign publications at random with Stanley knife and felt-tip pen. Universally loathed by ordinary Saudis, they are best given a wide berth.

Money

The riyal remains pegged to the US dollar at a rate of
SAR 3.75. All banks exchange dollars to riyals and the
other way round, as well as pounds sterling and euros
and some other currencies. There are also some
bureaux de change downtown, but they mostly target
Asian expatriates.

TIPPING

Saudis are generous tippers, perhaps to
compensate for the lack of respect with which
they tend to treat waiters. Staff in restaurants
(usually expatriates from the Middle East or Asia)
depend on tips to make ends meet, so it is a good
idea to leave a tip of at least SAR 5–10, even if that
amounts to more than 10 percent of the bill.

It's also good practice to tip the tea boys in
offices; they are often Sri Lankans who earn a
pittance and supplement their income by going
out to fetch food for you from a nearby shop or
making you an extra cup of coffee. A couple of
riyals per errand is about right. There is usually
an office collection for them on Eid al-Fitr: chip
in generously.

EATING OUT

Eating out is a popular pastime. In the Wahhabi
heartland, dining out with the family can be a

claustrophobic affair as curtains or partitions close tight around you; the family sections of more expensive restaurants in Jeddah and some upscale hotels elsewhere just have widely spaced tables in a separate part of the premises.

There is plenty of choice, the most common and reliable being Lebanese or Ottoman cuisine: kebabs and mezze including hummus, *mutabbal* (mashed eggplant), stuffed vine leaves, kofta, and all the delicious rest. The flavors tend to be milder than in the Mediterranean since the vegetables available here are bred for hardiness rather than flavor (that also goes for produce on sale in the supermarkets).

For a lunchtime snack, pick up a shawarma—chicken or lamb cut from the spit with spicy sauce and vegetables in a roll of flat bread—on any street corner. On the coast, simple restaurants let you choose a fresh fish that is then deep-fried and served with hummus, flat bread, and a rough salad. Upscale seafood restaurants offer a whole range of delicacies from mussels to lobsters, slow-baked or grilled.

Good, authentic Indian food is plentiful both in cheap eateries catering to South Asian laborers and in upscale North Indian places. The Filipino takeaways that dot Saudi cities tend to be heavy on congealing corn starch and knuckle bones and are perhaps best left to enthusiasts. Thai restaurants are a better alternative for East Asian flavors, even if not all the traditional ingredients are available.

There is also pricey Italian and even French food, though this tends to be bland since no wine is available for cooking.

Then of course there are fast food and "family" restaurants: every franchise under the sun is represented in the kingdom. Those who feel like reminding themselves how much starch, sugar, and Long Island dressing can be packed on a single plate have their opportunity in places like Hardee's and Chili's that can be hard to find outside the USA.

Traditional Arabian or Bedouin food can be more difficult to find, but there are some "heritage-experience" restaurants where you can try camel steak and interesting dishes of roast and stuffed lamb and chicken.

A whole chicken from the spit with rice can be had for SAR 10 in a little Afghan hole in the wall, while a full Lebanese feast in a baroque upscale eatery can cost many hundreds.

"SAUDI CHAMPAGNE"

"Saudi champagne" is a nonalcoholic punch of apple juice and sparkling water with plenty of fresh fruit chunks that makes a refreshing drink in the heat and goes surprisingly well with a meal. It's served in most of the better restaurants.

CAFÉ CULTURE

Coffee is of course a great Arabian tradition, and Saudis have a heroic tolerance for caffeine. Coffee shops are plentiful, serving excellent thimbles of thick Turkish coffee as well as Italian- and French-style brews with or without milk. Why Starbucks flourishes here is anyone's guess; perhaps it gives a sense of belonging to the wider world.

However, cafés up- and downtown, indoors and out, concentrate on *shisha*, sometimes with just a glass of tea (*chai*) on the side as an afterthought. In groups or alone, Saudis of all classes and ages love to relax with a *shisha*, topped up constantly by waiters running from table to table with their censers until it's time to go home. Whatever else Saudi Arabia may be, it's a smoker's paradise.

In the absence of alcohol, the *shisha* is the great social lubricant of the whole Middle East, with apple (*tufah*) only the most popular of many available tobacco flavors. Women are just as fond of puffing their *shishas* as men; pretty designs can spark fads, and thousands of riyals are spent on luxury models. Health and religious fanatics have naturally declared war on one of the last great Arabian traditions that still thrives here.

Even if the patrons in these *shisha* cafés are all *thobes* and bushy beards, nobody will bat an eyelid if a (male) Westerner sits down among them and does as they do. The point, after all, is to relax.

CULTURAL ACTIVITIES

Expatriates who enjoy reading should stock up on books before arriving in the kingdom. The big Jarir bookstore chain stocks mostly airport best sellers, and there is no guarantee that orders from Amazon.com will get past the censor or arrive within your lifetime. Magazines—and that includes arcane material such as the *Times Literary Supplement*—are habitually vandalized by the *mutawwa*, their guiding principles an eternal mystery. Perhaps, commentators speculate, it depends on the day of the week.

Due to the strict Islamic prohibition on the depiction of any living creature—and a general hostility among the establishment to most forms of artistic expression—contemporary art is limited to a few timid abstractions, invariably reminiscent of flowers, exhibited at a handful of liberal institutions and in business lobbies.

There is one exception. In the cautiously liberal days of King Faisal, Jeddah acquired a great deal of public statuary, including works by Henry Moore. Some of these are famous, like the giant bicycles and the moored boat in the middle of two landmark traffic circles. Others border on the *haram*, including one group of the signs of the zodiac and what can only be described as rearing horses.

Music is also frowned upon, though there are a few famous Saudi singers of opulent ballads that, as one long-term resident puts it, "start with *habibi* [my lover/love] and end with *habibi*." They can fill a sports stadium on the rare occasions when they perform. Traditional ensembles twang the *oud* (Arab lute) and beat the drum, but the music is mainly background accompaniment.

Foreign embassies and consulates occasionally organize cultural evenings, with lectures on the kingdom or film screenings. The best publication to find out about Arabian culture is *Saudi Aramco World*, the oil giant's in-house magazine whose guest writers are often international experts.

There are no cinemas, and films are roughly censored when they come out on video; a better option is downloading them on the Internet. Many people buy pirated copies in certain souks.

Historical Sites

The northern Arabian peninsula was home to the Nabateans, a mysterious tribe of bandits and traders who established a kingdom in the fourth century BCE that lasted until its defeat by the Roman emperor Trajan in 106 CE. As they grew in wealth and power, they dominated the trade routes in western Arabia from the East. Their capital was the amazing city of Petra, now in Jordan. The most significant Nabatean site in Saudi Arabia is Madain Salih. There, as at Petra, the giant palatial ruins hewn into the rock are actually tombs. Since it is in the desert, the site requires a two- or three-day trip.

Further south lies Jeddah's old town, or Balad, a square mile or so of distinctive buildings of coral limestone with jutting latticed balconies. Some of the buildings have been restored and admit visitors, others are home to mostly illegal immigrants and are falling to pieces, still others house shops and small businesses. A campaign to save this rare, almost intact historical townscape continues against massive odds.

In the Saudi heartland, there are the imposing fortresses of the rulers of the Najd, notably the Masmak fortress in Riyadh. In the deep south there are remnants of some impressive mud towns in the Yemeni style. Rock art survives in the Empty Quarter.

PICNICS

Saudis will picnic anywhere, including the median strip of the coastal highway. On Thursday evenings and on holiday nights, families crowd the sides of certain roads the way Northern Europeans throng the beaches of the Mediterranean—fully covered, of course. Seek out the pleasanter, leafier of the city parks or drive out into the desert for a more carbon dioxide-free experience under the stars.

DESERT TRIPS

A trip to the desert is essential to understanding Saudi Arabia. In this majestic silence, the snail's pace of life, the harsh certainties of religion, and

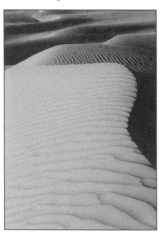

the lack of curiosity about the world can suddenly make sense. Thanks to the desert, lovers of off-road driving have a playground twice the size of Western Europe at their doorstep. The Empty Quarter, or Rub al-Khali, covers an area greater than France of—as the name suggests—nothing but rock and sand and salt flats. Spectacular sand dunes can rise over 984 feet (300 m). In the far east are quicksands that have allegedly swallowed entire caravans.

For more ambitious desert trips, it is vital to travel in groups. People still die out here when they get lost or run out of gas, even though highways now skirt or cross the wastes. Travel at least with two 4WD vehicles and never without a local guide. Drive off-road only if you are sure of your driving skills, and never too far. Carry more water and gas than you think necessary, and bring a shovel.

The best option is to book through a travel agency that specializes in such trips. Or drive on safe highways not too far out of the cities for a glimpse: even several miles out of town and a few hundred yards from the road, the experience can be breathtaking. Bear in mind that the nights can get very cold, so bring warm clothes and a sleeping bag.

SPORTS AND EXERCISE

The west coast has some of the best diving in the world, with unspoiled coral reefs stretching for miles up and down the coast from Jeddah. This is very popular among expatriates, and there are plenty of diving clubs. These are mostly found on private beaches that are also a convenient place to meet people—and where bathing in swimming trunks or a bikini is not a problem.

Saudis are great football enthusiasts, but the heat makes this an activity only for hardy types. Fitness clubs usually have tennis and squash courts and swimming pools as well as state-of-the-art gyms.

chapter seven

TRAVEL, HEALTH, & SAFETY

ROADS AND TRAFFIC

Oil being cheaper than water, Saudi Arabia is a country of cars. Roads are the kingdom's great pride. Main roads in the cities often have eight lanes or more, and well-maintained highways connect all the major points of the vast kingdom.

Traffic in the cities tends to clog at peak times,

but the jams are as nothing compared to megacities elsewhere in Asia. The real hazard is the way Saudis drive, swerving randomly across lanes and with total disregard for whoever follows behind, all the while swearing at anyone and everyone.

Road deaths top international statistics despite the fact that much of the kingdom is empty of people. Like everywhere in the world, except more so, people use their car to express their frustration and much else besides, even if it costs them their life.

LOCAL TRANSPORTATION

There is practically no mass transportation in the cities, though a few buses ply a handful of main routes. The oasis of efficiency that is Saudi Aramco in the Eastern Province runs its own buses, which connect the company's residential and industrial compounds and link them to Dhahran and al-Khobar.

The few people without their own car get around by taxi. These are white, can be flagged down anywhere, and have rather expensive meters that are never used. Instead, expect to agree upon a flat fare by distance, from SAR 10 to 20, rising to 30 for a trip across town. Most taxi drivers are from Pakistan or Egypt. Sit in the back or the driver may think you are sexually available, regardless of gender.

INTERCITY TRAVEL

The easiest way to get around the kingdom is by air. Saudi Arabian Airlines (Saudia) operates plenty of affordable daily flights between all the major and some minor cities.

For those with time on their hands, there are also air-conditioned buses connecting the major and minor cities. For trips to more out-of-the-way destinations, the best option is to fly to the nearest airport and rent a car.

ACCOMMODATION

Long-term

Accommodation for Western expatriates is usually in compounds, though villas and apartments are also easy to rent for those who fancy being closer to the everyday life of the cities. Compounds run the gamut from swank to very basic, but are popularly built in a sort of Canary-Island Andalusian style, like a retirement complex. They usually have plenty of facilities such as pools and gyms and offer freedom from many of the rules that restrict life outside—shops stay open at prayer times and the sexes can mingle freely.

Rent in a compound is several times as expensive as outside. This does not matter for Western expatriates who are put up by their employer, but it is a consideration if you are paid a housing allowance instead. Despite the heavy fortifications around the compounds, life in the cities is perfectly safe, and an apartment can be a good option for people who like to keep to themselves.

Apartments are classified for either families or "bachelors." Few are advertised, so the best option is to wander around an area you like and ask the superintendent, who can usually be found outside the building or somewhere on the ground floor. He may not speak English but will give you the landlord's number.

Short-term

Many major five-star chains have hotels in the big three centers of Riyadh, Jeddah, and al-Khobar–Dammam. Good independent hotels in more out-of-the-way destinations like al-Jouf can be booked through travel agencies. In the cities, there are also some hotels catering to ordinary Arab business travelers; though usually of a rather gloomy and forlorn appearance, they have perfectly adequate facilities.

Since there is practically no foreign tourism, there is no budget accommodation besides hostels for pilgrims from poorer countries, and they are best avoided.

HEALTH

Saudi Arabia is a very hot country. The coast is hot and humid, while inland is hot and dry, so drink plenty of bottled water to avoid dehydration and don't sit around in the midday sun. Food is usually safe to eat, though the odd bout of diarrhea is not unknown. Stock up on rehydration salt and Immodium. The sandstorms dry out the mucous membranes and tend to cause respiratory complaints.

To obtain a work permit, expatriates are legally required to produce a negative HIV test, but this is rarely enforced. The World Health Organization

(WHO) recommends vaccinations for diphtheria, measles, mumps, rubella, polio, and hepatitis B.

Health care in the many gleaming new hospitals is generally good. Doctors are either expatriates themselves or Saudis trained abroad. Nurses tend to be fearfully efficient Filipinos and Filipinas. Some doctors from other developing countries may rely excessively on antibiotics for minor ailments.

If you are here to work, your health insurance cover will come with a list of approved hospitals. Ask colleagues which one they favor. There is usually a flat fee of SAR 40 per visit to the doctor.

Pharmacies are plentiful and well stocked.

Outside the major cities, health care can sometimes be hard to find, so on excursions it is a good idea to keep a basic medical kit in the car.

SAFETY
Saudi Arabia is relatively free of violent and property crime. There are some clumsy scams, mostly targeting Asian expatriates, but on the whole the country is perfectly safe. However, it is best to avoid Islamist slums in the Wahhabi heartland, where religious zealotry and poverty combine to make Westerners unpopular.

Residential compounds and malls are exceedingly well guarded and the chances of falling victim to a terrorist attack are minuscule.

Male visitors of any age out walking may be alarmed when a car suddenly comes to a screeching halt next to them. Don't be: the driver is probably only going to proposition you for sex. Turn them down firmly if you're not interested—they can be persistent.

Western women alone in the back of their car may face some harassment from young men out driving and a certain amount of staring as they go about their shopping, but nothing like the ordeal Saudi women are subjected to. But the greatest danger of unpleasantness for women is probably from the authorities, including the *mutawwa*. Make sure you understand what restrictions apply in your area, wear an *abaya* in public, and keep a head scarf handy. Avoid the temptation to give the *mutawwa* a piece of your mind: only Egyptian women manage to get away with it.

BUSINESS BRIEFING

THE BUSINESS LANDSCAPE

As a gross simplification, Saudi Arabia's business landscape consists of a single giant oil corporation and a million small and medium-

sized enterprises, and nothing in between. There is little manufacturing of any kind— try finding goods labeled "made in Saudi Arabia" in a department store—but plenty of trading. In a desert country, nearly everything from daily necessities to the all-important cars has to be imported, meaning there are thousands of import businesses big and small. For millennia, Saudis have been traders rather than producers, but where caravans once slowly traversed the desert wastes, now ships, trucks, and airplanes do the heavy work.

Of course things have changed, and the rapid pace of development has especially favored construction companies, some of which, like the Bin Laden family's, have grown to mighty proportions. The communications revolution, meanwhile, has been a boon to media businesses: the *Al Arabiya* satellite channel is owned by a Saudi, and the pan-Arab daily *Asharq al-Awsat* is published from London by a Saudi prince.

These examples highlight another feature of the Saudi business landscape: almost all companies remain family businesses, and in the case of many larger businesses that family is the fifty-thousand-strong Al-Saud. The kingdom's richest individual businessman and owner of its tallest building is Prince Alwaleed ibn Talal.

The same is true even of ostensibly global businesses operating in Saudi Arabia: by law, they need a Saudi partner who owns more than 50 percent of the company and gets an equivalent share of the proceeds, from electronics giant LG (LG Shaker) to KFC. How the profits are actually divvied up, of course, is shrouded in mystery. In any case, what better partner to choose than a bona fide prince who is sure to shepherd his business partner safely through the bureaucracy?

A special case are Western defense contractors like Vinnell and British Aerospace, which employ large numbers of expatriates (often former military personnel, the so-called "lifers"), have their own company compounds, and generally keep to themselves, not least for security reasons.

Some foreigners do for all intents and purposes own businesses, especially corner shops: they circumvent the law by way of a sleeping Saudi partner. But most businesses are run by Saudis yet overwhelmingly staffed, down to the smallest mom-and-pop store, by foreigners.

SAUDI TIME

Arabs like to say that they think in terms of millennia rather than days or weeks, and that is certainly true for many business dealings, especially the processing of paperwork. But if things move at a snail's pace, they can also stagnate completely: it can sometimes seem to frustrated visitors that Saudis have a profound aversion to doing anything at all.

Yet this is not universal. Saudi banks, for example, process business at the same speed as elsewhere in the world. The difficulty is in telling the difference between slow progress and deliberate procrastination or inaction.

In other words, don't be afraid to prod. Do it politely, by asking, a couple of times, then with increasing firmness. Since face is important, it can sometimes be a good idea to find out who is really in charge and go directly to them—but be sure to give credit to the person who eventually claims it.

Getting Things Moving

Mr. Smith, an expatriate employee frustrated by the slow pace with which his paperwork was being processed, finally marched into the administration section of the firm and demanded action, only to be told that everything was ready but for the boss's signature. Smith offered to take the document to the boss himself but eventually agreed to wait another day. The following day, the boss called him into his office to announce that "the idiots" had finally done it. "I shouted at them . . . ," the boss claimed. Smith thanked him politely.

THE BUSINESS CULTURE

Hierarchy

Businesses are strictly hierarchical. The boss, who moves in mysterious ways, decides, and the chain of command is long. Within a company, Saudi and Asian staff are keenly conscious of their superior's greater status and manifest it in various expressions of respect both for his person and for the sanctity of his office.

If things take time, it is partly because every decision has to go through the entire chain of command—and the higher up the person on the ladder, the more license they have to be absent from the office for extended periods. Once visitors penetrate the inner sanctum, they may be struck to find that the desk, however vast, is completely bare except for a couple of telephones.

FLUNKEYS

Saudis of status love to surround themselves with underlings, preferably a whole entourage. Lower down the social scale this is usually a lone Asian expatriate; further up the ladder, the prize is other Saudis.

The editor-in-chief of one leading newspaper, for example, has a man called Hassan whose sole function is as a foil for the boss. Come to the chief with any request, and you will be told to "tell Hassan," who may or may not be present at the time. In fact, don't tell Hassan; there is nothing Hassan can or will do about it. Hassan is a bulwark, not a gateway, and the person to ask is someone else entirely.

This can be confusing when there are several underlings with no evident role milling about, as there tend to be. As a rule of thumb, the lone Indian among them is the man who really knows what's going on.

It was chiefly this obstinate survival of ancient feudal practice amid modern technology that for so long thwarted Saudi Arabia's perpetual attempts, announced roughly once a year with some fanfare, to join the World Trade Organization.

Connections

Personal relations are all-important, and that means hierarchies count. Any visitor wanting to strike a business deal in Saudi Arabia should seek to establish friendly ties with the man in charge. It can take time: no deal bigger than buying a packet of cigarettes was ever struck in a hurry in the kingdom.

This also explains that ubiquitous international figure, the Saudi middleman. From the notorious Adnan Khashoggi to the erstwhile ambassador to Washington, Prince Bandar ibn Sultan, these fixers have an important role to play in bringing people together.

More important still are connections in the Byzantine Saudi bureaucracy. Any transaction from getting a work permit to importing an airplane requires a mountain of paperwork, real or imagined, and must seemingly be processed through the entire official hierarchy, from desk to empty desk.

What Westerners might consider corruption, then, is often simply an extension of the Saudi culture of relationships and favors; nepotism, by the same token, is often inevitable given the sacred duty to look after one's juniors in the family network. Such practices have only recently been rooted out in the West, at least officially, and in the kingdom many of them are considered perfectly normal.

Wasta

Going through the regular channels is practically impossible, so *wasta*—clout or influence—is vital to get things done, either within the law or in circumvention of it. "If you have *wasta*," a student at a smart commercial college once told me, "the *mutawwa* will *bring* you drink."

Even for something simple like renewing a driver's license, there is a fellow outside the government office who for a very reasonable fee takes your papers to the right person. Ignore him at your peril. But by and large, foreigners who come to work in the kingdom have no choice but to put their trust in their employer's *wasta*, and businesspeople in their Saudi partner's.

BUSINESS ETIQUETTE
Tea
The great catalyst for establishing friendly relations in business is what Graham Greene called the

"ordeal by tea": glass after glass of black tea sweetened with at least two lumps of sugar, sometimes flavored with a leaf or two of mint, is drunk in offices almost nonstop, perhaps varied after evening prayer with a cup of strong Turkish coffee.

It would be rude to get straight to business. Arabs are world champions in shooting the breeze, so visitors and expatriates can expect to spend a considerable time chatting. Depending on your importance, your host may also answer phone calls, call in underlings to send them on errands, sign papers, and generally give the impression of being wonderfully busy. Don't be offended: the activity will probably cease the moment you are out of the office. Let your Saudi boss or business partner set the pace, unless it goes on for too long.

Even when there is a big meeting or negotiation with foreign visitors, it may be flanked by smaller, informal chats over tea in the boss's office. Again, the oddly democratic nature of Saudi society asserts itself here—a trace of tribal custom and the obligation of Islamic rulers to be available to hear their people's complaints.

Respect

Saudis and Asian expatriates show great respect for their superiors, standing up in the presence of the boss and addressing him as *Ustaz* (Master), a general term of respect for seniors in the Islamic world. However, this is not expected of Westerners; politeness will do. In fact, Saudis often seem to appreciate the lack of ceremony they believe to be common in the West, and may welcome the opportunity for a chat—perhaps in the manner of the kings of legend who disguised themselves as commoners to see what really went on in their realm.

A few young Saudis, still insecure because they have only recently attained the coveted status of *mudir*, may give themselves airs in your presence; but bear in mind that practically all Saudis have a somewhat regal demeanor.

It is polite to address Saudis by their title. If they have a Ph.D., be sure to call them "Doctor"; otherwise they are Mr., followed by the first name, e.g. Mr. Mohammed or Dr. Said. Hands are shaken at meeting and parting, but not across genders.

Remember that etiquette cuts both ways: while visitors should make all reasonable efforts not to offend their hosts, they need not put up with too much nonsense either. In certain contexts, especially with an employer or landlord, being firm can in turn establish the respect that is your due. Even a controlled loss of temper can sometimes work wonders in a culture where shouting is fairly common; but like everywhere else it should be a last resort.

Business Dress

Saudi men are properly dressed when they wear a *thobe* and sandals, though in many offices they wear closed shoes and socks; even those who otherwise dress in jeans and shirt for work will don a *thobe* for important meetings. Men of higher status often dress in particularly fresh, pressed *thobes*—the phrase "whiter than white" seems coined for them—and a white *ghutra* or *keffiyeh* instead of the common or checkered *shummagh*.

For Western men, a suit and tie or, if the heat won't permit, a long-sleeved shirt and tie are a must, together with closed shoes. For women, an *abaya* and token head covering. In a business situation, a visiting Western woman is unlikely to come into contact with a Saudi who insists that she be fully veiled in his presence.

MEETINGS

Saudis have warmed to the practice of exchanging business cards and will have theirs handy; so should visitors, to make the requisite impression of being someone of importance. Many business cards are printed in Arabic on one side and English on the other. Expatriates may be provided with such a card by their company. Be sure to check the information before giving the go-ahead for a print run of thousands.

Meetings—and certainly in-company meetings—usually proceed without a written agenda. The custom is for the senior Saudi, who will be seated at the head of the table, to speak at some length and then open the discussion to others. Take your cue from him.

Formal meetings start more or less on time and tend to get uncharacteristically straight down to business; punctuality—but not watch-tapping—is appreciated.

PRESENTATIONS

Presentations are becoming more common, especially in businesses that consider themselves international. Young, ambitious, foreign-educated office managers equip meeting rooms with all the gadgets, even if they are rarely used. Bear in mind, however, that middle managers are often foreigners themselves, who will go through the motions of a structured presentation—South Asians especially love a PowerPoint file—and expect the same from you.

In East and West, keep it brief. Saudis in particular drink a lot of coffee, and you may find it difficult to keep their attention for very long. Introductory jokes will fall flat, just as they do at home; there is no need to aim for any great entertainment value so long as the brevity imperative is observed.

Questions at the end, too, are likely to be more of a formality than an earnest search for enlightenment, and no one will try to catch the presenter out; the event is essentially for show and will have little impact on any negotiations or decisions that are eventually made elsewhere and on different grounds.

NEGOTIATIONS

It is rare for negotiations to be conducted in a single concentrated session. Rather, they will be a lengthy process around a centerpiece formal meeting, or meetings, of the two sides. That process also includes informal chats over tea in the office and the intercession of third parties who will have a word in this or that ear. Bring time, or better still prepare to make several trips.

That is not to say that the big meeting, when it comes, will not have to be thoroughly prepared. An even temper and a sense of humor are of the essence, and any 1980s-style macho approach would completely alienate your hosts. Saudis prefer to feel comfortable with a business partner.

Yet charm and leisurely pace apart, their initial demands may well be outrageous; adjust your own strategy accordingly and expect to inch cordially toward common ground from widely divergent positions. Arabs, incidentally, are fond of throwing their hands up in dismay and appealing to the heavens for patience. Usually this is a good-natured pantomime and might even be worth copying.

CONTRACTS AND FULFILLMENT

A contract is a statement of where you stand at the moment that remains endlessly negotiable, for both sides. It is the relationship that counts, not the piece of paper. Honor certainly requires that a man's word is his bond, and in extreme cases an appeal to a business partner's honor may be in order; otherwise, the key is to keep Saudi partners engaged. Keep in touch and maintain an exchange of friendly tokens. A long silence can be more deadly for a business relationship than a heated argument.

The same goes for the employment contracts of Western expatriates. They can of course expect to be paid on time, in full, and should tolerate no delays. But any other issues are open to renegotiation without a new document needing to be drawn up. Never fear: Saudi employers are extremely unlikely to dishonor the new agreement. In fact, due to the patron–client relationships Saudis like to maintain, Western expats often find that the reality of their employment is more favorable than the paper contract stipulates.

SETTLING DISPUTES

In disputes, it is a good idea to blame third parties or fate rather than a Saudi partner, even if it is clear to both sides who is really at fault. If the fault is yours, however, Saudis will value a sincere apology, partly because it comes so hard to them if the shoe is on the other foot.

Even in serious disputes, it is worth trying to work things out informally rather than resorting to lawyers. Don't be afraid to use all the political and acting skills at your disposal, from wheedling to tantrums to going behind a man's back to someone who is likely to pass on the message. But whatever you do, don't insult your Saudi partner face-to-face. Once a disagreement is settled, Saudis will often act as if nothing has happened.

The law—that is, the commercial or labor courts—should be the last resort. There are conflicting reports about their efficacy.

SOCIALIZING

Saudis are hospitable people and will put on a generous spread for important business visitors, preferably in a five-star hotel. New employees are also often taken out for a meal by their boss. There are special occasions—something like office Christmas parties back home but rather more sober—where companies invite their staff and families to a hotel, upscale restaurant, or catered event. A favorite is the lavish *suhour* feast in the small hours during Ramadan.

Such events are informal, enjoyable, and well worth attending, but there is none of the compulsion of a country like Japan, where failure to show is practically a sackable offense. Dressing neatly in a shirt and tie is appreciated.

For those who have come to work for a company, there are also opportunities to go out for dinner with colleagues from many different backgrounds. Those in a position of responsibility could do worse than take out their Asian colleagues (who probably earn far less) for a meal on some occasion important to Westerners, such as Christmas.

WOMEN IN BUSINESS

Women make up a mere 5 percent of the labor force but half the university graduates. There are a number of prominent Saudi businesswomen, almost invariably from the leading liberal merchant families of the Hijaz or associated with

Saudi Aramco; whether they are breaking a mold or exist in a bubble afforded them by their privileged background is as yet unclear, but the kingdom is certainly keen to put the money that often lies idle in women's bank accounts to work (see page 68).

In the end, the chances are that the pressures of the market will win the day. And if Saudi Arabia is ever to end its reliance on foreign expertise, it will need to put its highly educated and, more to the point, motivated young women to work: the men have proved that they can't do it alone.

chapter **nine**

COMMUNICATING

LANGUAGE

Arabic is a flowery language, full of sweeping generalizations and sometimes extravagant hyperbole. Arabs often express their own position, at great volume, through virulent denunciations of the slightly different. Thus when an Arab says, "We will drive you into the sea," he may only mean, "I don't entirely agree with you."

In an argument, Arabs paradoxically use violent language to preempt physical confrontation. The shouting can go on for a long time without degenerating into fisticuffs, unless it gets so bad that the next step is murder. One advantage for visitors, as we have seen, is that a controlled loss of temper, after a suitable period of waiting to get things done, can work wonders.

Exaggeration is also the driving force of much Arab humor. The government spokesman who said, "Not even my own mother talks to me honestly" (see page 107), and the student's, "If you have the right connections, the *mutawwa* will *bring* you drink" (see page 146) are examples.

Many Saudis speak English fluently, often

because they have lived or been educated abroad, though they may write it with difficulty. The young elite sometimes speak better English than Arabic and love to show off to foreigners—cue "Yo, man" and other such borrowed slang. French is also sometimes spoken among the upper classes, especially the older generation.

Learning Arabic

Foreigners who make the effort to learn Arabic find that it opens a new world for them, both in practical understanding and in emotional rewards from their hosts. The Saudis are often touchingly grateful for efforts to understand their culture.

The spoken language is the Gulf dialect, with its soft "g"s and rounded long "a"s, while the written language throughout the Arab world is classical Arabic. TV presenters use a spoken form of classical Arabic. If you want to learn the language, sign up for colloquial Arabic first, or make sure the instructor isn't going to teach from the Koran—of very little use in everyday life.

MANNERS

Saudi manners are a strange mixture of the gracious and the rude. To venture a theory, when a Saudi can't recognize a clearly defined social relationship with another, he feels no obligations at all. Thus a host will behave with great generosity and warmth to a guest, but the same man will push and shove his way in front of another in the bakery line and unleash a torrent of invective when the other person objects.

While most Saudis now live in big cities, their development is so recent that civic values have not yet found a way into the collective consciousness. There is no neighborliness, no responsibility for public space, no sense of community based on a shared habitat. Rampant littering, with whole truckloads dumped by the roadside at night, is one manifestation of this.

This is one reason it can be difficult to meet Saudis socially: there is simply no appropriate Bedouin value for dealing with total strangers except *in extremis*. In a small town, you may be graciously welcomed by a man of importance, but in the cities no one feels they have a stake in the larger community. If you make the effort to build a relationship—going from "occasional customer" to "honored guest in my establishment," say—the monosyllabic shopkeeper of yesterday can metamorphose into a warm, gregarious host.

And then, underneath the sometimes regal bearing and the loud talk (there is a sense that talking loudly signals strength and talking quietly indecision), Saudis are shy. Once they overcome their suspicion of strangers, they can become alarmingly trusting: Saudi Arabia remains a gold mine for con men, scroungers, and charlatans, especially when they don an Islamic cloak.

It's important to treat elders with respect and return a greeting in kind. There can of course be no public displays of affection, though married Saudi couples are allowed to hold hands. The politest way for a man to treat a women he doesn't know well is to ignore her. Men hug and kiss each other on the cheek when they meet. Social encounters can end quite abruptly.

Non-Muslim visitors should tread carefully in matters of religion, but Saudis love debating everything under the sun including their government, which they may denounce vehemently even while doing nothing about it.

BODY LANGUAGE

Saudis fidget, forever playing with their worry beads, jiggling their feet, and craning in all directions. This does not usually mean they are bored with your conversation; it probably only means they've had too much caffeine.

On first meeting, Saudis give strangers a searching stare that can be a little unsettling. But after that, they avoid eye contact, meaning that visitors from Anglo-Saxon or northern European countries may feel more comfortable here than elsewhere in the Middle East or Mediterranean.

To express respect, an underling may remain standing in the presence of his seated betters. Polite young people perch upright at the edge of their chair in the presence of their elders, and it would be rude to slump in your chair when sitting with someone of great age. But Saudis love to lounge, and among roughly equals and long-term familiars, they tend to sprawl comfortably on the cushions any way they like.

It's rude to point the soles of your feet at someone you are with, because they are in contact with the unclean ground (by extension, slapping someone with a shoe is an expression of utter contempt), but that doesn't apply to people at the next table in a café, for example, who are outside the social circle.

SERVICES
Telephones
Saudi Telecom's landlines usually work perfectly well both within the kingdom and for international calls. For cell phones, international calls remain expensive: shop around for an affordable package if you call outside the country a lot. Cell phones are ubiquitous, including among the Bedouin in the desert, and this has had a huge social impact. Camera phones are banned in the

kingdom, apparently for fear that men could use them to take pictures of women.

For the still phone-less, which generally means low-paid expatriate laborers, there are businesses with individual cubicles where you can call home at all hours except prayer times.

EMERGENCY PHONE NUMBERS	
Ambulance	997
Fire	998
Police	999
Traffic Accidents	993

Mail

Postal services are reliable, at least as far as sending things abroad is concerned. Letters from abroad usually arrive within a week. A problem is the absence of proper addresses: few houses have numbers, and many still take the form of "third house behind the mosque on the left." Use your office address unless you live in a well-known compound. DHL and UPI are available, at a price.

Incoming packages are inspected and, if found offensive, censored or confiscated by the authorities. Placing an order for books or DVDs from abroad is a pointless gamble. Magazine subscriptions usually get through, if not always on time, but may well be defaced.

THE MEDIA
Newspapers

The press is tightly controlled by the government. Saudi Arabia's leading Arabic papers include the mass circulation *Okaz*, whose often fanciful and lurid reports and unrivaled access to police work make it the closest the country has to a tabloid newspaper, and the reform-minded *Al-Watan*. Sports papers are also hugely popular—the joke goes that they're the only ones that tell the truth.

The kingdom has two English-language newspapers, *Arab News* and the *Saudi Gazette*, which offer a good selection of international wire reports often attributed to partly or wholly fictitious correspondents. They also carry a smattering of local news, puffs for the paper's advertisers and the cronies of the editors-in-chief, plus blow-by-blow accounts of the internal feuds of the big expatriate communities.

Owned by a close associate of Interior Minister Prince Naif, the *Saudi Gazette* has better access to local crime stories, but the English leaves a lot to be desired. *Arab News*, whose editor-in-chief is in the king's camp, has some interesting local and regional columnists—and excellent pages on the subcontinent, many written by genuine correspondents. Both are in effect run (and self-censored) by Indians and are in no way representative of the kingdom.

Some international newspapers and magazines are available (with excisions) in the big bookstores and (without) on the Internet.

TV and Radio

Saudi VHF/UHF TV broadcasts officially controlled news, often in the form of announcements from the Saudi Press Agency, as well as Islamic programs and some entertainment including talk shows. It also has a dreary English-language channel, mostly broadcasting silent goings-on from within some royal palace or programs of Islamic edification.

Most Saudis therefore rely on satellite access, depending for news on Al Jazeera and Al Arabiya, which are usually quicker to report stories from inside the kingdom. Dishes can be picked up easily in the souks, and so can vendors of illegal decoder cards that unlock some two hundred channels. They are trustworthy and will come to your home and do the necessary for a very reasonable fee. The practice is so widespread that there is no need to fear repercussions.

Radio remains popular in-car entertainment. Local and national channels broadcast a mix of discussion and educational programs that rely heavily on Islam. For classic rock and news bulletins in short, simple sentences, there is AFN.

INTERNET

King Abdul Aziz City for Science and Technology
(KAIST), which operates the Internet, is a giant
censorship operation that blocks millions of Web
sites. Many are blocked automatically, triggered for
example by prompts like "sex" as in "Middlesex
University" and similar foolishness. Proxy servers to
circumvent these blocks are therefore a vital tool for
any surfer; since they slow down the connection, users
should make sure to get a fast one in the first place.

CONCLUSION

Saudi Arabia may seem a subdued, even dull place
from a distance; but on closer acquaintance it emerges
as a fascinating country, not only because of its vital
political and cultural importance in the international
arena, but also because of its people. Reticent but, on
closer acquaintance, charming and warm hosts, the
Saudis form a far less monolithic society than one
might expect. Their gift for storytelling, their humor,
and their endurance leave a lasting impression.
Finally, no short introductory book can provide a
substitute for experiencing the awe-inspiring silence
of the kingdom's deserts for yourself.

Further Reading

Alireza, Miriam. *At the Drop of a Veil*. Boston: Houghton Mifflin, [1971] 1991.

Alsanea, Rajaa. *Girls of Riyadh*. London: Penguin, 2007.

Armstrong, Karen. *Islam: A Short History* (revised). New York: Modern Library, 2002.

Bradley, John R. *Saudi Arabia Exposed: Inside a Kingdom in Crisis*. New York: Palgrave Macmillan, 2005.

Ham, Anthony et al. *Saudi Arabia*. Melbourne: Lonely Planet Publications, 2004.

Lawrence, T. E. *Seven Pillars of Wisdom: a Triumph*. London: Penguin, [1926] 2000.

Long, David E. *Culture and Customs of Saudi Arabia*. Westport: Greenwood Press, 2005.

Al-Rasheed, Madawi. *A History of Saudi Arabia*. Cambridge: Cambridge University Press, 2002.

Thesiger, Wilfred. *Arabian Sands*. London: Longmans, 1959.

Complete Arabic: The Basics. New York: Living Language, 2005.

In-Flight Arabic. New York: Living Language, 2001.

Index